Common Core

Standards for Mathematical Content

Domain Counting and Cardinality

Cluster Know number names and the count sequence.

Cluster Count to tell the number of objects.

Cluster Comparing numbers.

Standards K.CC.3, K.CC.4, K.CC.4.b, K.CC.4.c, K.CC.5, K.CC.6

Standards for Mathematical Practice

- ✔ Make sense of problems and persevere in solving them.
- ✔ Reason abstractly and quantitatively.
- ✔ Construct viable arguments and critique the reasoning of others.
- ✔ Model with mathematics.
- ✔ Use appropriate tools strategically.
- ✔ Attend to precision.
- ✔ Look for and make use of structure.
- ✔ Look for and express regularity in repeated reasoning.

Comparing and Ordering 0 to 5

Planning

Lessons

Review and Assessment

Pearson, Scott Foresman, Pearson Scott Foresman, and enVisionMATH are trademarks, in the U.S. and/or in other countries, of Pearson Education Inc., or its affiliates.

Common Core State Standards: © Copyright 2010. National Governors Association Center for Best Practices and Council of Chief State School Officers. All rights reserved.

"Understanding by Design" is registered as a trademark with the United States Patent and Trademark Office by the Association for Supervision of Curriculum Development (ASCD). ASCD claims exclusive trademark rights in the terms "Understanding by Design" and the abbreviation "UbD".

Pearson Education has incorporated the concepts of the Understanding by Design methodology into this text in consultation with [contributing author/editor] Grant Wiggins, [one of the] creator[s] of the Understanding by Design methodology. The Association for Supervision of Curriculum Development (ASCD), publisher of the "Understanding by Design Handbook" co-authored by Grant Wiggins, has not authorized, approved or sponsored this work and is in no way affiliated with Pearson or its products.

ISBN-13: 978-0-328-67324-7
ISBN-10: 0-328-67324-2

4 5 6 7 8 9 10 V003 15 14 13 12 11

BIG IDEA Comparison and Relationships Numbers, expressions, measures, and objects can be compared and related to other numbers, expressions, measures, and objects in different ways.

ESSENTIAL UNDERSTANDINGS

2-1 If you compare two groups of objects and the number of objects match, the groups have the same number of objects. If one group has items left over, that group has more. The other group has fewer objects.

2-2 *1 more than* or *2 more than* expresses the relationship between two groups of objects.

2-3 *1 fewer than* or *2 fewer than* expresses the relationship between two groups of objects.

2-4, 2-5 Zero is a number that tells how many objects there are when there are none.

2-6 If you compare two groups of objects and the number of objects match, the groups have the same number of objects. If you compare two groups and one group has items left over, that group has more. The other group has fewer objects.

2-7 There is a specific order to the set of whole numbers. Zero is a number that tells how many objects there are when there are none.

BIG IDEA Number Uses, Classification, and Representation Numbers can be used for different purposes, and numbers can be classified and represented in different ways.

ESSENTIAL UNDERSTANDING

2-8 Numbers can be used to tell order (ordinal numbers). Positions/order in a row can be found by counting, and ordinal names are similar to number names.

BIG IDEA Practices, Processes, and Proficiencies Mathematics content and practices can be applied to solve problems.

ESSENTIAL UNDERSTANDING

2-9 Some problems can be solved by using objects to act out the actions in the problem.

Comparing Groups

Equal Groups

Before developing understanding of language for specific numbers, young children can identify and create equivalent groups by matching each object in one group with exactly one object from a second group. In the action of matching, or one-to-one correspondence, all the attributes, such as color, position, and size, must be ignored, and the formal idea of number emerges. If the objects in two groups match one-to-one, then a child recognizes that the two groups have the same quantity of objects, although the child may not know the number name to use to describe that quantity.

Children may describe the idea of number by saying that there are "just as many" forks as plates or that they each have "the same number" of crayons.

More and Fewer

More and Fewer

Based on the understanding of equal quantities, young children can compare groups to determine whether one group has more or fewer elements than another group and can create a group that has one more or one fewer than a given group. Children draw on these experiences with relative size to order numbers sequentially as they begin to learn number names and symbols.

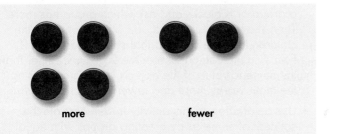

more   fewer

Ⓒ Mathematical Practices: Model with Mathematics

In *more* and *fewer* lessons, reinforce the concept by modeling groups that have obvious differences in amounts, such as 5 counters and 20 counters.

Point out to children that when we add 1 more or 2 more to a group, the group gets bigger. To reinforce this concept, add objects to groups 1 or 2 objects at a time, and then have children compare the first group with the last group.

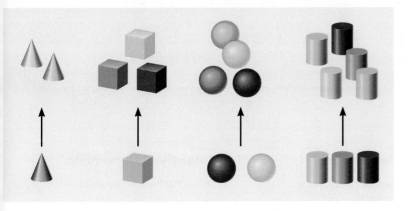

Numbers to 5

Number Relationships

Children can apply their skills of counting, comparing groups, and recognizing one more to order the numbers through 5. As they connect their knowledge of the counting sequence and the relative values of the quantities, they can answer such questions as, "Which number comes before 3?" and "Which number comes after 4?"

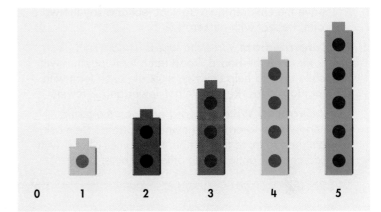

0   1   2   3   4   5

Ⓒ Mathematical Practices: Use Tools

To reinforce the sequence of numbers through 5, use stacking blocks to illustrate that the sequence of numbers represents an increase in quantity.

For a complete list of *enVisionMATH* Professional Development resources in print, on DVD, and online, see the *Teacher's Program Overview.*

ELL

ELL STRATEGY Use Repetition

Considerations for ELL Children

Repeated oral language practice of terms will help English learners remember the words and associate them with concepts.

- **Beginning** Write the numeral 1 on the board and have the children hold up 1 object and say the word *one*. Repeat with numerals 2–5.
- **Intermediate** Write the words *1 more* and *2 more* on the board. Read each term together with children and help children illustrate each term with manipulatives. Repeat with *1 fewer* and *2 fewer*.
- **Advanced** Write the word *order* on the board. Model how to order the numerals 0 to 5. Then ask children to trace the number that comes after 4 with red chalk. Continue with other numbers.

Special Needs

RTI

Considerations for Special Needs Children

- Review with children the concept of *more, fewer,* and *same*.
- Using various manipulatives, demonstrate these concepts and ask the children to replicate your model. For example, show a group of 2 blocks and a group of 8 blocks and ask which group has more. Then show another group of 2 objects and ask the children to make a group that shows more than 2. Focus on the comparison of the 2 groups, rather than the numeric value of the objects in the group, using the math words *more* and *fewer* to describe them.
- Use a variation of this activity to demonstrate the concept of *same as* by creating groups with equal numbers of objects.

Below Level

RTI

Considerations for Below Level Children

- Help children understand that they can build on the concepts of *equal groups* and *more* introduced in Topic 2.
- Show a group of objects such as 4 cubes. Model for children how to make a group that has *1 more* object than another group, or *1 fewer* object.
- Provide numerous opportunities for children to practice making groups that have *1 more, 2 more, 1 fewer,* and *2 fewer*.

Advanced/Gifted

Considerations for Advanced/Gifted Children

- Children who quickly relate quantity to number will understand that 3 cubes and 3 dogs are both 3, no matter the item.
- Write 2 different numbers from 0 to 5 on the board. Ask children to draw sets of dots for the numbers and then circle the larger number.

Response to Intervention

RTI TIER 1 ONGOING	**Ongoing Intervention**	RTI TIER 2 STRATEGIC	**Strategic Intervention**	RTI TIER 3 INTENSIVE	**Intensive Intervention**
	• Lessons with guiding questions to assess understanding • Support to prevent misconceptions and to reteach		• Targeted to small groups who need more support • Easy to implement		• Instruction to accelerate progress • Instruction focused on foundational skills

Reading Comprehension and Problem Solving

Ⓒ Use Structure:

Using Reading Comprehension Strategies

Even when math problems are presented using a picture book format, a good reading comprehension strategy to use in math problem solving is using objects to act out problems.

Questions to Guide Comprehension

Use these comprehension questions with the Guided Practice Exercises in Lesson 2-9. *What do we need to find out?* [Which group of stickers has the fewest.] *What do you know?* [There are 3 snake stickers, 2 flamingo stickers, and 5 fish stickers.]

Act It Out! *How can you use cube trains to solve the problem?* Give each child 10 connecting cubes. Have children make cube trains to show how many stickers are in each group.

Talk It Out! *How can you tell a story problem while you act it out?* Help children make up a story problem about most and fewest. For example, *[Child's name] has 3 snake stickers. How can [she/he] show the stickers?* [Make a cube train with 3 cubes.] *[Child's name] has 2 flamingo stickers. How can [she/he] show the stickers?* [Make a cube train with 2 cubes.] *[Child's name] has 5 fish stickers. How can [she/he] show the stickers?* [Make a cube train with 5 cubes.]

Draw It Out! *How can you draw a picture of the problem?* Children can draw cube trains to show the groups of stickers and compare the lengths of cube trains.

Lesson 2-9, Guided Practice

Vocabulary Activities

1 Fewer, 1 More

Ⓒ **Attend to Precision** Draw a group of 4 circles on chart paper. Ask children to draw a group with 1 fewer. Repeat with a group of 4 circles and 1 more. Have children use their vocabulary cards *1 fewer* and *1 more* to label the drawings. Continue with 2 more and 2 fewer.

1 fewer (than)

1 more (than)

Math and Literature

MathStart™

Just Enough Carrots by Stuart J. Murphy helps children to understand the concept of greater, lesser, and same amounts through a story about various animals shopping for food items. For activity suggestions for this book see *Guided Problem Solving for the Math Library*.

Writing Center

What's the Order?

Materials
Paper with numbers out of order, markers

- Prepare sheets of paper by writing numbers 0 to 5 in a row, and display them out of order, such as 4, 1, 3, 0, 2, 5.
- Each child takes a sheet of paper and then rewrites the numbers in order.

Science Center

Watch Them Grow

Materials
Clear plastic cups, wet paper towels, small beans, black marker, masking tape

- Tell children they will plant beans and watch them grow. Assign each child a number from 1 to 5. Have them write the number on a piece of masking tape and stick it onto a cup.
- Have children moisten a paper towel and place it in the cup. They can take their number of beans and put them in the cup between the paper towel and the side of the cup.
- Have children put their cups in order according to their number labels.
- As the plants grow, children can count the number of sprouts and compare them with the number of seeds in each cup. *Which has more? Which has fewer?*

Movement Center

Giant Steps or Not?

Materials
Masking tape or chalk

- On the floor, use masking tape or chalk to make an 8-foot line.
- Have children walk from the beginning to the end of the line taking no more than 5 steps.
- Vary the game by having children walk the line by taking fewer than 4 steps, more than 5 steps, 2 more steps than 3, and so on.

Math Center

Ordering Numbers

Materials
Small bags, Number Cards 0–5 (Teaching Tool 5), paper clips, small objects to place in bags (blocks, clips, marbles)

- In one bag place 1 object, another bag, 2 objects, and so on; one bag should have nothing in it.
- Have children fasten number cards to the bags.
- Then they put the bags in order from 0 to 5.

Dramatic Play Center

Yummy Fruit!

Materials
Plastic fruit or vegetables, sticky notes, 2 clear plastic bags

- Give each child a bag containing 5 pieces of plastic fruit. Partner A chooses some pieces of fruit from his or her bag, counts them, tells how many there are, and writes the number on a sticky note. Partner A then says to Partner B: "Show 1 fewer" or "Show 2 fewer."
- Partner B counts pieces of fruit to show 1 or 2 fewer and writes the number on a sticky note. Partner A tells whether he or she agrees with the number.
- Partners reverse roles and repeat the activity.

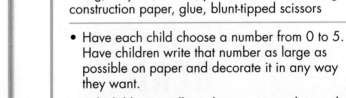

Art Center

Tasty Number Ordering

Materials
String, crayons, straws, pasta, beans, buttons, glitter, construction paper, glue, blunt-tipped scissors

- Have each child choose a number from 0 to 5. Have children write that number as large as possible on paper and decorate it in any way they want.
- Ask children to tell you how to group the numbers and then display their work in order on a bulletin board.

I am Anna

This is a story in which children compare 2 groups of objects and decide which group has more or fewer.

1 ▶ **Before the Story**

Picture Walk

Hold up the book and read the title, author's name, and illustrator's name to the children. *Do you think this story takes place at home or school?* [School] *How can you tell?* [There are things that are in school such as the alphabet, bulletin board, and blocks.] *Who is the main character in this story?* [Anna]

Activate Prior Knowledge

In this story we will count with Anna to find out which group of objects has more or fewer. Hold up 4 crayons and 2 pencils. *Do I have more or fewer crayons?* [More] *How many more?* [2 more] *Which do I have fewer of, pencils or crayons?* [I have fewer pencils than crayons.]

This book belongs to:

Suzanne

Topic 2 Story

I am Anna
Written by Diane Brown   Illustrated by Rémy Simard

h Ii Jj Kk Ll Mm Nn Oo Pp Qq

I see hooks.
I see coats.
I see more   .

Topic 2   **1**

I see hats.
I see shoes.
I see fewer

Topic 2   **2**

2 ▶ **During the Story**

READ

Read the story aloud for enjoyment. Then read each page aloud and wait for children to respond to the text. Do they, like Anna, see more or fewer than each group of objects? Have them answer orally and then circle their answer.

GESTURE

Have children point to and count aloud the number of hooks (1, 2, 3, 4, 5) and coats (1, 2). Read aloud the sentences on the page. Have children circle the answer to the last statement with fingers (hooks). Summarize by saying: *5 hooks is more than 2 coats. 5 hooks is 3 more than 2 coats.* Do the same with the groups on the remaining pages.

I see mops.
I see brooms.
I see more _____.

Topic 2 3

I see green blocks.
I see blue blocks.
I see yellow blocks.
I see fewer _____.

Topic 2 4

fold down

Extension

Have partners work together to gather 2 groups of objects such as blocks, books, toys, crayons, or pencils. Have the partners present their 2 groups to classmates. Have them tell the number in each group and which group has more (fewer) and how many more (fewer).

You may wish to have children take home their Interactive Math Story book and share what they have learned about more and fewer.

COLOR

Distribute the Interactive Math Story books to children. On page 1, have children color 5 letters of the alphabet red and 2 blue. *Are there more or fewer red letters?* [More] On page 3, have children color the mops gray and the brooms brown. On page 4, have children color the blocks on the top shelf green, the blocks on the middle shelf blue, and the blocks on the bottom shelves yellow.

WRITE

Revisit the first page of the story. Count the 5 hooks aloud with the children, then write 5 on the board. Have children write 5 next to the sentence "I see hooks." Then have them count the number of coats (2), write the number on the board, and have children write it next to "I see coats."

SPEAK

Invite children to retell the story in their own words, starting with "Anna sees …." Encourage children to talk about the other pictures included on the pages: the toys, artwork, stove.

Review What You Know

Purpose
Diagnose children's readiness by assessing prerequisite content.

Understanding by Design

Children will be able to answer the Topic Essential Question by the end of the topic. Revisit the question throughout the topic. Then use the Topic 2 Performance Assessment. The question relates to a Unifying Concept.

Topic Essential Question

• How can numbers from 0 to 5 be compared and ordered?

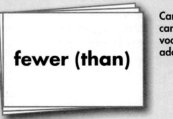

Cards can always be used as flash cards. Have children create large vocabulary cards with visuals to add to the classroom word wall.

"Understanding by Design" is registered as a trademark with the Patent and Trademark Office by the Association for Supervision of Curriculum Development (ASCD). ASCD has not authorized, approved or sponsored this work and is in no way affiliated with Pearson or its products.

School Fun

What You Need
12 counters
paper clip
pencil

Number of Players: 2
How to Play
1. Take turns. Spin the spinner. Say the number.
2. Place a counter on a group in the picture that is made up of that number of people or objects.
3. Play until all the groups are covered.

Topic 2   twenty-two   22

Game
for school or home

Purpose
Provide children with an opportunity to practice prerequisite skills. Before they begin the game, you may wish to discuss with children the numerals 2, 3, and 4 and review the corresponding quantities for each. Ask the children to look at the spinner and point to each of the numerals as you say them with the children.

Math Project

Social Studies

Directions
Show the children a picture of 2 orange blossoms, or use 2 real flowers. Ask the children to look at the picture (or flowers) and draw a picture that shows 1 more flower.

Write the numerals 2 and 3 on the board and read them with the children. Have children match the numerals on the board with the pictures.

More, Fewer, and Same As

 **Quick and Easy** Lesson Overview

Objective	Essential Understanding	Vocabulary	Materials
Children will use one-to-one correspondence to compare objects and decide whether one group has *more*, *fewer*, or the *same number as* the other group.	If you compare two groups of objects and the number of objects match, the groups have the same number of objects. If one group has items left over, that group has more. The other group has fewer objects.	**more** (than) **fewer** (than) **same as** **same number of** **column** **row**	Connecting cubes

Domain
Counting and Cardinality

Cluster
Comparing numbers.

Standard
K.CC.6 Identify whether the number of objects in one group is greater than, less than, or equal to the number of objects in another group, e.g., by using matching and counting strategies.

© PROFESSIONAL DEVELOPMENT

Math Background

In this lesson, children use what they know about equal groups to compare groups that have more and fewer objects. Children need to utilize the concept of one-to-one correspondence (matching objects in one group to objects in another group) to see that there will be objects left over.

Mathematical Practices

☑ Make sense of problems and persevere in solving them.

☑ Reason abstractly and quantitatively.

☑ Construct viable arguments and critique the reasoning of others.

○ Model with mathematics.

☑ Use appropriate tools strategically.

☑ Attend to precision.

○ Look for and make use of structure.

☑ Look for and express regularity in repeated reasoning.

1 Daily Common Core Review

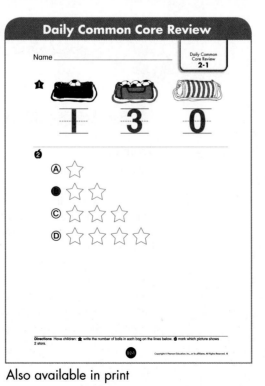

Content Reviewed

Exercise 1   Use Numbers to Tell How Many

Exercise 2   Count Objects

Also available in print

30 min # Problem-Based Interactive Learning
Hands-On
Minds-On

Overview Children will make and compare groups to determine which group has more, fewer, or the same number as another group.

Focus How does using one-to-one correspondence help you compare two sets of objects?

Materials Connecting cubes

Vocabulary **more** (than), **fewer** (than), **same as**, **same number of**, **column**, **row**

Set the Purpose Remind children that they have learned that numbers tell how many. *You will learn how to compare groups of objects in this lesson.*

Connect *Do we have a chair for every child in our class? Do we have extra chairs, or chairs left over? How could we find out?*

MATHEMATICAL
PRACTICES

Make Sense of Problems
Ask children how they can use one-to-one correspondence to help them compare two sets of objects.

Academic Vocabulary Point out to children that the words **more**, **fewer**, **same as**, and **same number of** are often used to compare two groups of objects. Hold up 4 cubes. *Who can show me a group of cubes that has more than this group? The same as this group? Fewer cubes than this group?*

Pose the Problem *Anna is very happy. She started kindergarten today. She sees boys and girls. Are there more boys than girls in her class?* Have children share their ideas about how to find the answer.

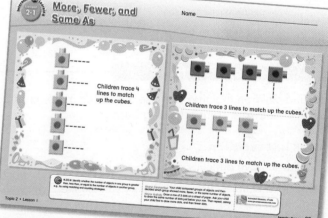

Model Move 5 yellow cubes in a **column** onto the workmat to show the girls Anna sees in her kindergarten class. Have children do the same, as you point out the column of cubes. *Anna sees boys in the room. Place 4 blue cubes on the workmat. Now trace the top line from your yellow cube on the left. Place a blue cube next to the line you traced. Now trace the next line and place another cube next to that line.* Continue until children have placed 2 more cubes. Point to the column of 5 yellow cubes. *Look at the cubes you placed for the girls on the left. Now look at the blue cubes you placed for the boys on the right. Which group has more?* [Yellow cubes] *How do you know?* [There is 1 cube left over.] *Are there more boys or girls?* [Girls]

Small Group Interaction Have partners work together to complete the **rows** of cubes on the right side of the student page. Have children listen to this story: *Anna now sees 4 trucks in the block corner. She sees 3 cars too. Which group shows fewer objects?* Continue: *Anna sees 3 paintbrushes. Anna sees 3 easels.*

Extend *What other ways can we use to find out which group has more, fewer, or the same number?* [Count, draw a picture, or match up items.]

eTools **Counters**
www.pearsonsuccessnet.com

Visual Learning

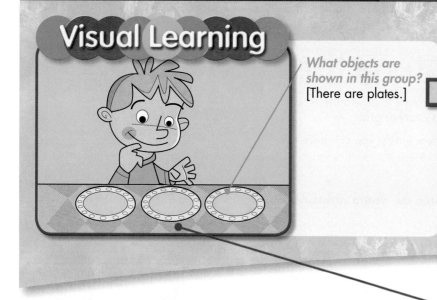

What objects are shown in this group? [There are plates.]

What is different about the groups of objects in this box? Are there more plates or more forks? How do you know? [There are more forks because one is left over.]

1 Visual Learning

Set the Purpose Call attention to the **Visual Learning Bridge** at the top of the page. *In this lesson, you will learn about when to use the math words more, fewer, or same as.*

Animated Glossary Children can see highlighted words defined in the Online Student Edition.

more (than), **fewer** (than), **same as**, **same number of**, **column**, **row**

www.pearsonsuccessnet.com

2 Guided Practice

Remind children that they can use the words *more, fewer,* and *same as* when they are comparing 2 groups of objects.

Error Intervention

If children have difficulty drawing the lines,

then have children use craft sticks to match the 2 groups.

Do you understand? *How can you find out which group of objects has more?* [Match the objects one-to-one and if 1 group has some left over, it has more.]

Reteaching Make a row of 5 children and a row of 3 children facing each other. Ask children who don't have partners to raise their hands. Then describe this row as having more children than the other row, which has fewer. Have the 2 children without partners move away so that one row has the same as the other.

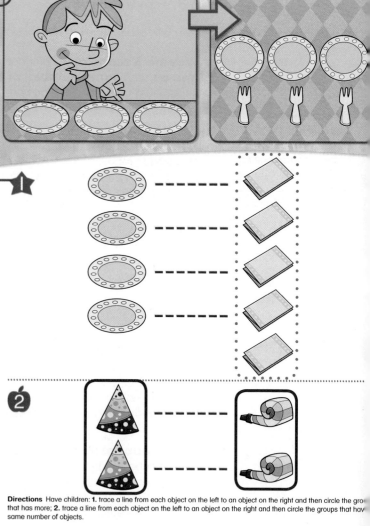

Directions Have children: **1.** trace a line from each object on the left to an object on the right and then circle the group that has more; **2.** trace a line from each object on the left to an object on the right and then circle the groups that have same number of objects.

Topic 2 • Lesson 1

What objects are in each group? [There is a group of plates and a group of forks.] *Are there more plates, more forks, or the same number of each?* [They have the same number.] *How do you know?* [They match up one-to-one.]

Are there more or fewer forks? How do you know? [There are fewer forks because there is one plate left over.]

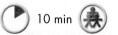

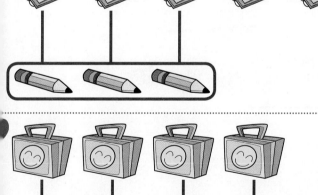

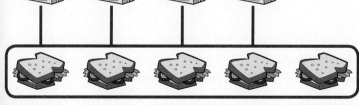

tions Have children draw a line from each object in the top row to an object in the bottom row and then: **3.** circle the ┐up that has fewer; **4.** circle the group that has more.

twenty-four **24**

Additional Activity

Big Chairs and Little Blocks

🕐 10 min 👥

Materials 5 small blocks, 5 chairs, 5 pieces of string

- Line up a row of 5 blocks and a row of 2 chairs.
- Have children walk around each row and look at the objects. Then have children connect a block and a chair with string, making the 2 possible pairs.
- Question children to determine which row has more or fewer objects than the other. Add 3 chairs to the chair row and have children connect the new pairs with string to show the *same as*.
- Repeat by varying the number of objects in each row.

3 **Independent Practice**

Children draw lines to match 2 groups of objects. They circle the group of objects that has fewer (Exercise 3) or more (Exercise 4).

Close

Essential Understanding If you compare two groups of objects and the number of objects match, the groups have the same number of objects. If one group has items left over, that group has more. The other group has fewer objects. *Remember to match up objects so you can tell which group has* more, *which has* fewer, *and which has the* same number.

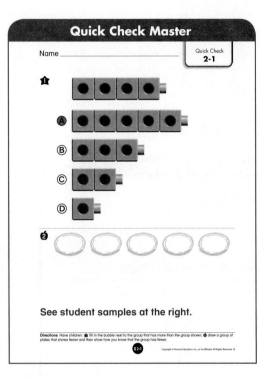

Quick Check Master

Name _____

Quick Check
2-1

☆

Ⓐ

Ⓑ

Ⓒ

Ⓓ

②

See student samples at the right.

Directions Have children: ☆ fill in the bubble next to the group that has more than the group shown; ② draw a group of plates that shows fewer and then show how you know that the group has fewer.

02-1 Copyright © Pearson Education, Inc., or its affiliates. All Rights Reserved. K

Formative Assessment

Use the **Quick Check** to assess children's understanding.

ⓒ **ASSESSMENT**

Exercise 1 is worth 1 point.
Use the rubric to score Exercise 2.

Exercise 2

Use Appropriate Tools Children should be able to draw to show a group with fewer objects.

ⒺⓁⓁ **Rephrase** For children who need additional help following directions, rephrase a question or statement in a different way, rather than repeating it.

Student Samples
3-point answer Children draw up to 4 plates and draw lines to show one-to-one correspondence.

2-point answer Children draw up to 4 plates but do not draw lines to show one-to-one correspondence.

1-point answer Children color in 1 to 4 plates but do not draw any other pictures to show a group that has fewer.

Prescription for Differentiated Instruction
Use children's work on the **Quick Check** to prescribe differentiated instruction.

Points	Prescription
0–2	Intervention
3	On-Level
4	Advanced

Differentiated Instruction

Intervention

Special Delivery

⏱ 10 min 🧑‍🤝‍🧑

Materials (per pair) Yellow and green color tiles, 2 envelopes, paper strips

• Put 4 yellow tiles in one envelope and 3 green tiles in the other.

• Each child takes an envelope, empties out the tiles, and lines them up opposite each other. Children then use strips to show one-to-one correspondence between tiles.

• Have partners decide who has *more* tiles and who has *fewer*. Ask them to use additional tiles so that one row is the *same as* the other row.

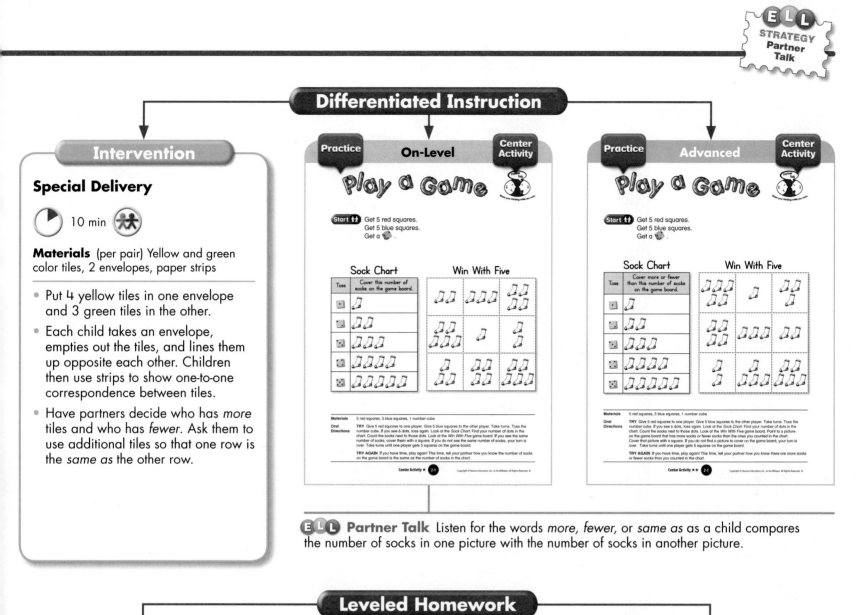

Practice — **On-Level** — **Center Activity**

Play a Game

Advanced

Play a Game

ELL Partner Talk Listen for the words *more, fewer,* or *same as* as a child compares the number of socks in one picture with the number of socks in another picture.

Leveled Homework

Reteaching Master

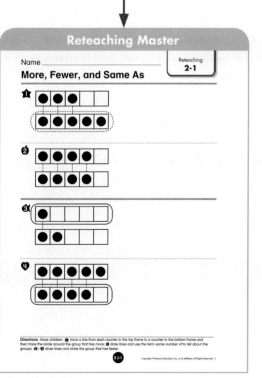

Practice Master

Enrichment Master

Also available in print

Also available in print

Also available in print

DIGITAL eTools **Counters**
www.pearsonsuccessnet.com

DIGITAL eTools **Counters**
www.pearsonsuccessnet.com

DIGITAL eTools **Counters**
www.pearsonsuccessnet.com

24C

1 and 2 More

Common Core

Domain
Counting and Cardinality

Cluster
Comparing numbers

Standard
K.CC.6 Identify whether the number of objects in one group is greater than, less than, or equal to the number of objects in another group, e.g., by using matching and counting strategies.

Mathematical Practices

☑ Make sense of problems and persevere in solving them.

☑ Reason abstractly and quantitatively.

○ Construct viable arguments and critique the reasoning of others.

○ Model with mathematics.

☑ Use appropriate tools strategically.

○ Attend to precision.

○ Look for and make use of structure.

☑ Look for and express regularity in repeated reasoning.

 **Lesson Overview**

Objective	Essential Understanding	Vocabulary	Materials
Children will recognize and identify a group of objects that has *1 more* or *2 more* than another group.	*1 more than* or *2 more than* expresses the relationship between two groups of objects.	**1 more** (than) **2 more** (than)	Connecting cubes, crayons, Writing Practice 4, 5, 0 (Teaching Tool 13)

PROFESSIONAL DEVELOPMENT

Math Background

Research says ... children will build on the concepts of equal groups and more introduced in Lesson 2-1. Knowing numbers that are 1 more than or 2 more than another number without counting is useful in many situations (Van de Walle & Watkins, 1993).

1 Daily Common Core Review

Daily Common Core Review 2-2

Directions Have children mark the best answer. ★ Are there more dogs, cats, or birds? Circle your answer. ❷ Which number tells how many ducks?

Also available in print

Content Reviewed

Exercise 1   Identify More Than, Less Than
Exercise 2   Use Numbers to Tell How Many

 30 min # Problem-Based Interactive Learning

Overview Children will find the group of objects that is 1 more or 2 more than another group.

Focus How can you tell whether a group has 1 more or 2 more?

Materials Connecting cubes, crayons

Vocabulary **1 more** (than), **2 more** (than)

- -

 **Engage**

Set the Purpose Remind children that they have learned how to compare groups of objects. *You will learn to show different numbers of objects in groups in this lesson.*

Connect Display a group of 3 cubes and a group of 4 cubes. *Which group has more cubes?* [Group of 4 cubes] Show a group of 4 cubes and 2 cubes. *Which group has more cubes?* [Group of 4 cubes]

- -

 MATHEMATICAL PRACTICES

Reason Abstractly
Ask children how they would compare groups of objects to find out which group has more.

Academic Vocabulary Explain that the terms **1 more** and **2 more** can be used when comparing 2 groups of objects. Use cubes to model. *If I had 2 red crayons and 3 blue crayons, would I have 1 more blue crayon or 2 more blue crayons?* [1 more]

Pose the Problem *Anna's teacher puts 5 cups in a row on a table. Then she puts 4 napkins in a row on the table. How can we show which group has 1 more than the other group?* Have children share their ideas.

Model Move 5 blue cubes in a horizontal row onto the workmat as children do the same. *Now I will show the group of napkins by putting 4 red cubes in the row below the blue cubes.* Have children do the same. *Which group of cubes shows 1 more?* [Blue] *How do you know?* [There is 1 blue cube left over.] *Now trace and color blue in each square for each blue cube you have on the workmat. Color each square red for each red cube you have. Which row shows 1 more?* [Blue row] *Now Anna's teacher puts 5 napkins and 3 cups on a table.* Continue to model as above to teach 2 more.

Use Math Manipulatives Make sure children place their cubes directly below one another for one-to-one correspondence.

Small Group Interaction Have partners work together to complete the student page as they listen to more stories about Anna's teacher. *Anna's teacher puts 3 books on the table and 4 crayons.* Continue: *Anna's teacher puts 3 juice boxes on the table and 1 pitcher of milk.*

- -

Extend

Show 3 cubes in a row and have children count them. *How many cubes would I have if I put 2 more cubes in the row?*

 DIGITAL eTools **Counters** www.pearsonsuccessnet.com

Visual Learning

How many cubes do you see? [1] Model telling a story about Anna and 1 cube. Then have volunteers tell their own stories to the class. *Anna wants to make rows of cubes. She starts with a row of 1 cube.*

Anna is holding another row of cubes. How many cubes are in this row? [2 cubes] *Which row has more cubes?* [The one she is holding.] *How many more cubes are in the row Anna is holding?* [1 more]

1 Visual Learning

Set the Purpose Call attention to the **Visual Learning Bridge** at the top of the page. *In this lesson, you will learn when you can use the terms 1 more and 2 more to describe groups of objects.*

Animated Glossary Children can see highlighted words defined in the Online Student Edition.
1 more (than), **2 more** (than)
www.pearsonsuccessnet.com

2 Guided Practice

Remind children that they can match up objects to decide which group has 1 more or 2 more objects.

Error Intervention

If children have difficulty comparing groups of objects,

then have them draw lines to match objects one-to-one and then trace the objects.

Do you understand? *Do you have to count to know which group has one more or two more?* [No, you can match up each object and then tell.]

Reteaching Make two stacks of 2 connecting cubes each and explain that each stack has the same number of cubes. Add a cube to one stack and discuss what happens when one stack has 1 more than the other. Add another cube to the same stack and discuss what happens when one stack has 2 more than the other.

Directions Have children: **1.** color in yo-yos to show 1 more; **2.** color in basketballs to show 2 more.

Topic 2 • Lesson 2

Anna wants to make other rows of cubes. How many cubes are in this row? [2]

Anna is holding another row of cubes. How many cubes are in this row? [4 cubes] Which row has more cubes? [The one that Anna is holding.] How many more cubes? [2 more] What would you do to find out which row has more? [Count or match up each cube one-to-one.]

Check children's drawings:

5 sandwiches

5 apples

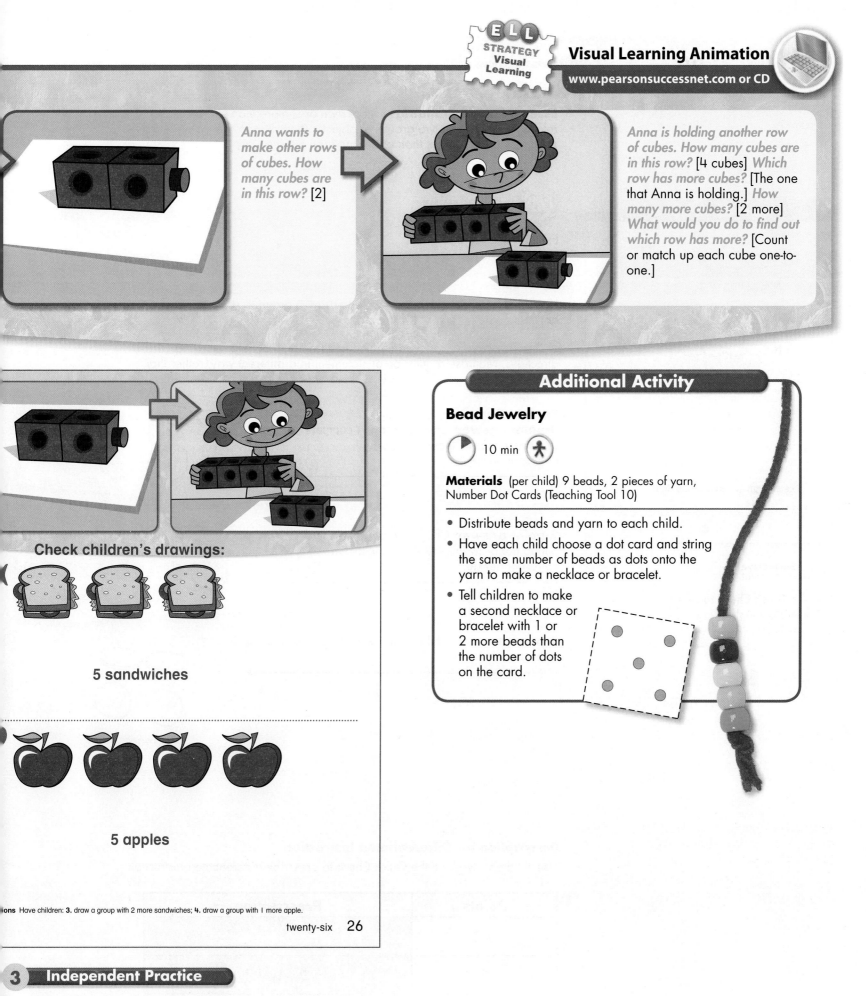

Additional Activity

Bead Jewelry

⏱ 10 min 🚶

Materials (per child) 9 beads, 2 pieces of yarn, Number Dot Cards (Teaching Tool 10)

- Distribute beads and yarn to each child.
- Have each child choose a dot card and string the same number of beads as dots onto the yarn to make a necklace or bracelet.
- Tell children to make a second necklace or bracelet with 1 or 2 more beads than the number of dots on the card.

ons Have children: **3.** draw a group with 2 more sandwiches; **4.** draw a group with 1 more apple.

twenty-six **26**

3   Independent Practice

Children draw a group with 2 more sandwiches and a group with 1 more apple.

Close

Essential Understanding *1 more than* or *2 more than* expresses the relationship between two groups of objects. *Remember to match up objects to see if there is 1 more than or 2 more than another group.*

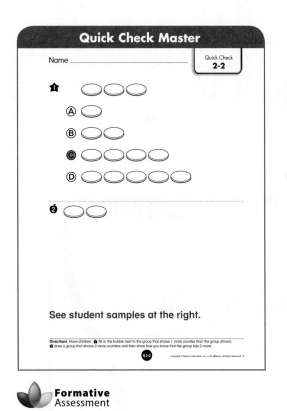
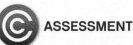

Formative Assessment

Use the **Quick Check** to assess children's understanding.

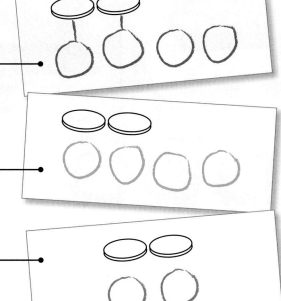

ASSESSMENT

Exercise 1 is worth 1 point.
Use the rubric to score Exercise 2.

Exercise 2

Use Tools Children should be able to draw a group to show 2 more objects.

ELL Rephrase For children who need additional help following directions, rephrase a question or statement in a different way, rather than repeating it.

Student Samples
3-point answer Children draw 4 counters and draw lines to show one-to-one correspondence.

2-point answer Children draw 4 counters but do not draw lines to show one-to-one correspondence.

1-point answer Children draw a group that is the same.

Prescription for Differentiated Instruction
Use children's work on the **Quick Check** to prescribe differentiated instruction.

Points	Prescription
0–2	Intervention
3	On-Level
4	Advanced

Differentiated Instruction

Intervention

One More

🕐 10 min 👥

Materials Connecting cubes, small objects (blocks, crayons)

- Have one partner place any number of objects in a row.
- Have the other partner put down a cube for each object, plus 1 more cube.
- To verify that the second group has 1 more, have children match the cubes to the objects one-to-one by placing them side-by-side.
- Repeat by partners switching roles.

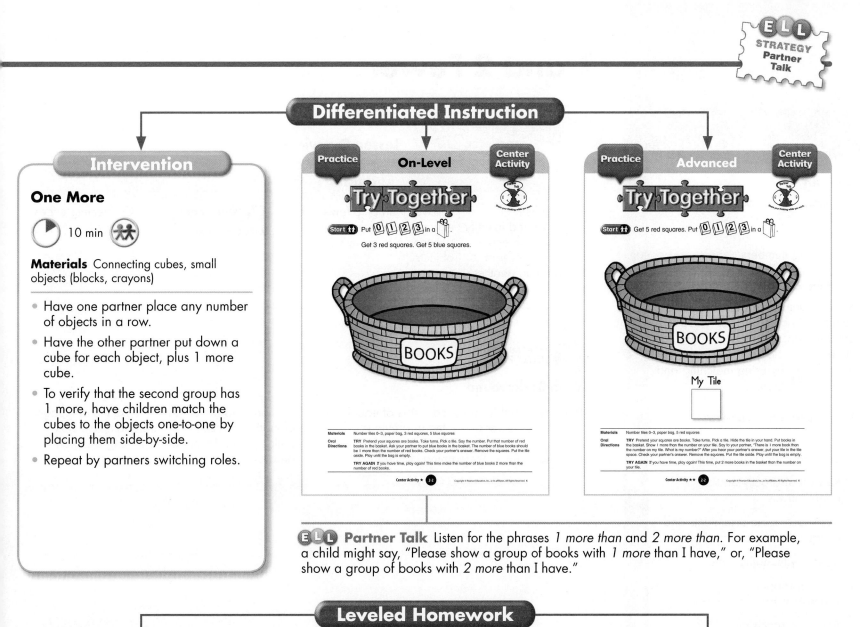

Practice — On-Level — **Center Activity**

Try Together

Start 👣 Put 0 1 2 3 in a 👜.

Get 3 red squares. Get 5 blue squares.

BOOKS

Materials — Number tiles 0–3, paper bag, 3 red squares, 5 blue squares

Oral Directions — **TRY** Pretend your squares are books. Take turns. Pick a tile. Say the number. Put that number of red books in the basket. Ask your partner to put blue books in the basket. The number of blue books should be 1 more than the number of red books. Check your partner's answer. Remove the squares. Put the tile aside. Play until the bag is empty.

TRY AGAIN If you have time, play again! This time make the number of blue books 2 more than the number of red books.

Center Activity ★ 2-2   Copyright © Pearson Education, Inc., or its affiliates. All Rights Reserved. K

Practice — Advanced — **Center Activity**

Try Together

Start 👣 Get 5 red squares. Put 0 1 2 3 in a 👜.

BOOKS

My Tile
[ ]

Materials — Number tiles 0–3, paper bag, 5 red squares

Oral Directions — **TRY** Pretend your squares are books. Take turns. Pick a tile. Hide the tile in your hand. Put books in the basket. Show 1 more than the number on your tile. Say to your partner, "There is 1 more book than the number on my tile. What is my number?" After you hear your partner's answer, put your tile in the tile space. Check your partner's answer. Remove the squares. Put the tile aside. Play until the bag is empty.

TRY AGAIN If you have time, play again! This time, put 2 more books in the basket than the number on your tile.

Center Activity ★★ 2-2   Copyright © Pearson Education, Inc., or its affiliates. All Rights Reserved. K

ELL Partner Talk Listen for the phrases *1 more than* and *2 more than*. For example, a child might say, "Please show a group of books with *1 more* than I have," or, "Please show a group of books with *2 more* than I have."

Leveled Homework

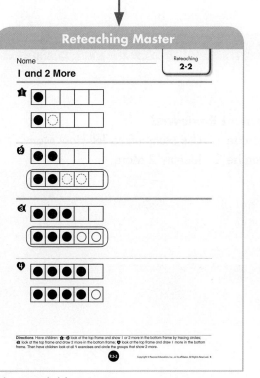

Reteaching Master

Name _____   Reteaching **2-2**

1 and 2 More

Directions Have children: ★–❷ look at the top frame and show 1 or 2 more in the bottom frame by tracing circles; ❸ look at the top frame and draw 2 more in the bottom frame; ❹ look at the top frame and draw 1 more in the bottom frame. Then have children look at all 4 exercises and circle the groups that show 2 more.

R 2-2   Copyright © Pearson Education, Inc., or its affiliates. All Rights Reserved. K

Also available in print

Practice Master

Name _____   Practice **2-2**

1 and 2 More

🍌🍌 banana

🥪🥪 sandwich

🍊🍊🍊 orange orange

🧁 muffin muffin

Directions Have children: ★ draw 1 more banana; ❷ draw 1 more sandwich; ❸ draw 2 more oranges; ❹ draw 2 more muffins. Then have children tell about each row of pictures using the terms 1 more or 2 more.

P 2-2   Copyright © Pearson Education, Inc., or its affiliates. All Rights Reserved. K

Also available in print

Enrichment Master

Name _____   Enrichment **2-2**

Stripes and Spots

Check children's drawings for accuracy.

Directions Have children draw 1 more stripe on the kitten's fur, draw 2 more stripes on the mother cat, draw 2 more spots on the grown dalmatian dog, and draw 1 more spot on the dalmatian puppy.

E 2-2   Copyright © Pearson Education, Inc., or its affiliates. All Rights Reserved. K

Also available in print

DIGITAL eTools **Counters** www.pearsonsuccessnet.com

DIGITAL eTools **Counters** www.pearsonsuccessnet.com

DIGITAL eTools **Counters** www.pearsonsuccessnet.com

Domain
Counting and Cardinality

Cluster
Comparing numbers

Standard
K.CC.6 Identify whether the number of objects in one group is greater than, less than, or equal to the number of objects in another group, e.g., by using matching and counting strategies.

Mathematical Practices

✔ Make sense of problems and persevere in solving them.

✔ Reason abstractly and quantitatively.

○ Construct viable arguments and critique the reasoning of others.

○ Model with mathematics.

✔ Use appropriate tools strategically.

✔ Attend to precision.

○ Look for and make use of structure.

✔ Look for and express regularity in repeated reasoning.

1 and 2 Fewer

Quick and Easy Lesson Overview

Objective	Essential Understanding	Vocabulary	Materials
Children will recognize and identify a group of objects that has *1 fewer* or *2 fewer* than another group.	*1 fewer than* or *2 fewer than* expresses the relationship between two groups of objects.	**1 fewer** (than) **2 fewer** (than)	Connecting cubes, crayons

© **PROFESSIONAL DEVELOPMENT**

Math Background

This lesson builds on the concepts of equal groups and fewer presented in previous lessons. Relative value is an important concept of number sense. By learning concepts such as more and fewer, children use the language of mathematics to compare quantities. This builds a foundation for beginning addition and subtraction.

1 Daily Common Core Review

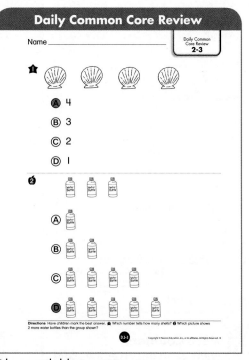

Content Reviewed

Exercise 1 Use Numbers to Tell How Many
Exercise 2 Identify 2 More

Also available in print

 30 min # Problem-Based Interactive Learning

 Hands-On Minds-On

Overview Children will find the group of objects that is 1 fewer or 2 fewer than another group.

Focus How can you tell whether a group has 1 fewer or 2 fewer?

Materials Connecting cubes, crayons

Vocabulary **1 fewer** (than), **2 fewer** (than)

 Engage

Set the Purpose Remind children that they have learned how to compare groups of objects. *You will learn to show different numbers of objects in groups in this lesson.*

Connect Show children a group of 5 cubes and a group of 4 cubes. Ask which group has fewer cubes. Then show a group of 3 cubes and 5 cubes. *Which group has fewer cubes? What did you do to find out which group has fewer?* [Children could count or match up the cubes.]

MATHEMATICAL
PRACTICES

Reason Abstractly
Ask children how they could compare groups of objects to tell which group has fewer.

Academic Vocabulary Explain that the terms **1 fewer** and **2 fewer** can be used when comparing 2 groups of objects. Use cubes to model. *If I had 1 red and 3 blue crayons, would I have 2 fewer blue crayons or 2 fewer red crayons?* [2 fewer red crayons]

Pose the Problem *George's teacher puts 4 paintbrushes on the table. Then she puts 5 paint jars on the table. How can we tell which group has 1 fewer object?* Have children share their ideas.

Model Move 4 green cubes in a horizontal row onto the workmat as children do the same. *Now I will show the group of paint jars by putting 5 yellow cubes in the row below the green cubes.* Have children do the same. *Which group of cubes shows 1 fewer?* [Green] *How do you know?* [There is 1 yellow cube left over.] *Now color in each square green for each green cube you have on the workmat. Color in each square yellow for each yellow cube you have. Which row shows 1 fewer?* [Green row] *Now George's teacher puts 2 paintbrushes in a row and 4 paint jars on a table.* Continue to model as above to teach 2 fewer.

Small Group Interaction Have partners work together to complete the student page as they listen to more stories about George's teacher. *George's teacher puts 1 book on the table and 2 crayons.* Continue: *George's teacher puts 5 milk cartons on a table and 3 cups.*

 Extend

Draw 2 balls on the board. *How many balls would there be if there were 2 fewer?* [0]

DIGITAL
eTools **Counters**
www.pearsonsuccessnet.com

Visual Learning

How many cubes do you see? [4] Model telling a story about George and 4 cubes. Then have volunteers tell their own stories to the class. *George wants to make rows of cubes. He starts with a row of 4 cubes.*

George is holding another row of cubes. How many cubes are in this row? [3 cubes] *How many fewer cubes are in the row George is holding?* [1 fewer] *How do you know?* [By matching one-to-one or counting]

1 Visual Learning

Set the Purpose Call attention to the **Visual Learning Bridge** at the top of the page. *In this lesson, you will learn when you can use the terms* 1 fewer *and* 2 fewer *to describe groups of objects.*

Animated Glossary Children can see highlighted words defined in the Online Student Edition.
1 fewer (than), **2 fewer** (than)
www.pearsonsuccessnet.com

2 Guided Practice

Remind children that they can match up objects to decide which group has 1 fewer or 2 fewer objects.

Error Intervention

If children have difficulty comparing groups of objects,

then have them draw lines to match objects one-to-one and then trace the objects.

Do you understand? *Do you have to count to know which group has 1 fewer or 2 fewer?* [No, you can match up each object and then tell.]

Reteaching Line up 2 rows of 4 beans each and match each one-to-one. Then take 1 bean away and ask children to describe the groups. Repeat with different numbers of beans. Then take 2 beans away from the rows and repeat.

Directions Have children: **1.** color cars to show 1 fewer; **2.** color party horns to show 2 fewer.

Topic 2 • Lesson 3

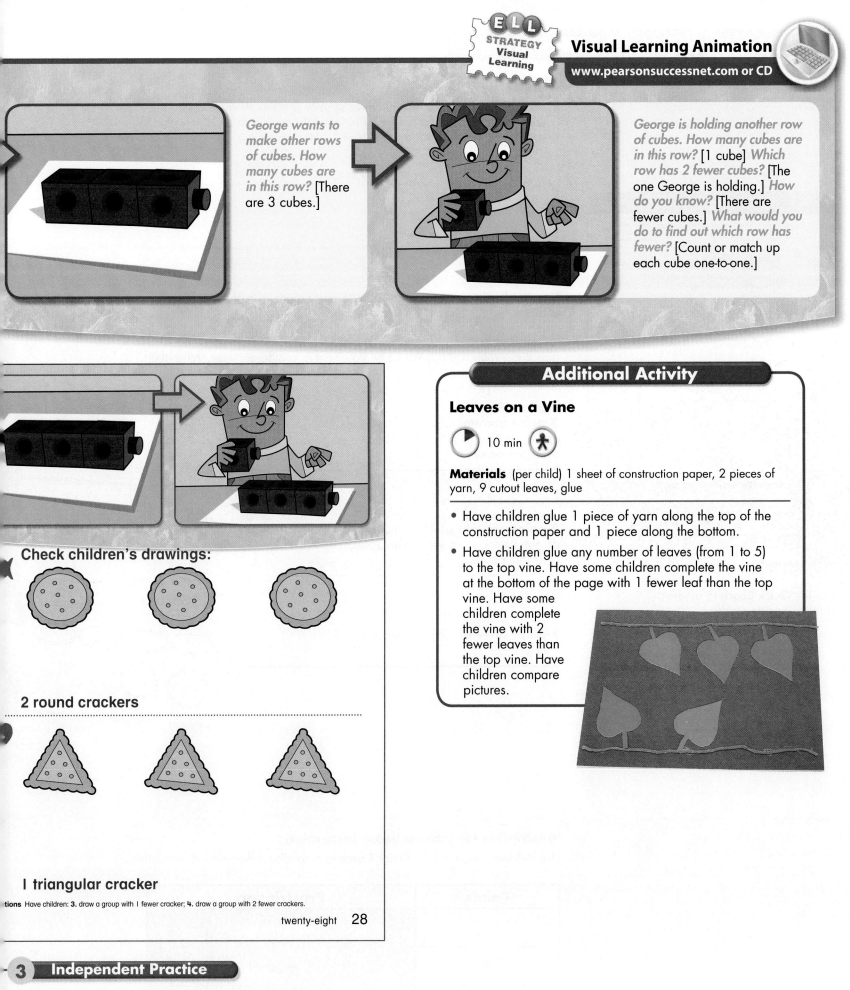

George wants to make other rows of cubes. How many cubes are in this row? [There are 3 cubes.]

George is holding another row of cubes. How many cubes are in this row? [1 cube] *Which row has 2 fewer cubes?* [The one George is holding.] *How do you know?* [There are fewer cubes.] *What would you do to find out which row has fewer?* [Count or match up each cube one-to-one.]

Check children's drawings:

2 round crackers

1 triangular cracker

tions Have children: **3.** draw a group with 1 fewer cracker; **4.** draw a group with 2 fewer crackers.

twenty-eight 28

Additional Activity

Leaves on a Vine

🕐 10 min 👤

Materials (per child) 1 sheet of construction paper, 2 pieces of yarn, 9 cutout leaves, glue

- Have children glue 1 piece of yarn along the top of the construction paper and 1 piece along the bottom.

- Have children glue any number of leaves (from 1 to 5) to the top vine. Have some children complete the vine at the bottom of the page with 1 fewer leaf than the top vine. Have some children complete the vine with 2 fewer leaves than the top vine. Have children compare pictures.

3 **Independent Practice**

Children draw a group with 1 fewer cracker and a group with 2 fewer crackers.

Close

Essential Understanding *1 fewer than or 2 fewer than expresses the* relationship between two groups of objects. *Remember to match up objects to see if there is 1 fewer than or 2 fewer than another group.*

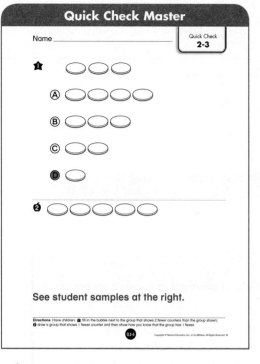

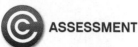

Formative Assessment

Use the **Quick Check** to assess children's understanding.

 ASSESSMENT

Exercise 1 is worth 1 point.
Use the rubric to score Exercise 2.

Exercise 2

Use Tools Children should be able to draw a group to show 1 fewer object.

E L L Rephrase For children who need additional help following directions, rephrase a question or statement in a different way, rather than repeating it.

Student Samples
3-point answer Children draw 4 counters and draw lines to show one-to-one correspondence.

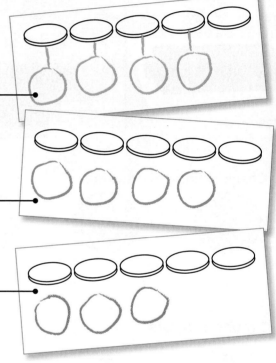

2-point answer Children draw 4 counters but do not draw lines to show one-to-one correspondence.

1-point answer Children draw 1 to 3 counters.

Prescription for Differentiated Instruction
Use children's work on the **Quick Check** to prescribe differentiated instruction.

Points	Prescription
0–2	Intervention
3	On-Level
4	Advanced

Differentiated Instruction

Intervention

Two Fewer

🕐 10 min 👥

Materials Connecting cubes, small objects (blocks, crayons)

- Have one partner place any number of objects in a row.
- Have the other partner put down 2 fewer connecting cubes.
- To verify that the second group has 2 fewer, have children match the cubes to the objects one-to-one by placing them side-by-side.
- Repeat by partners switching roles.

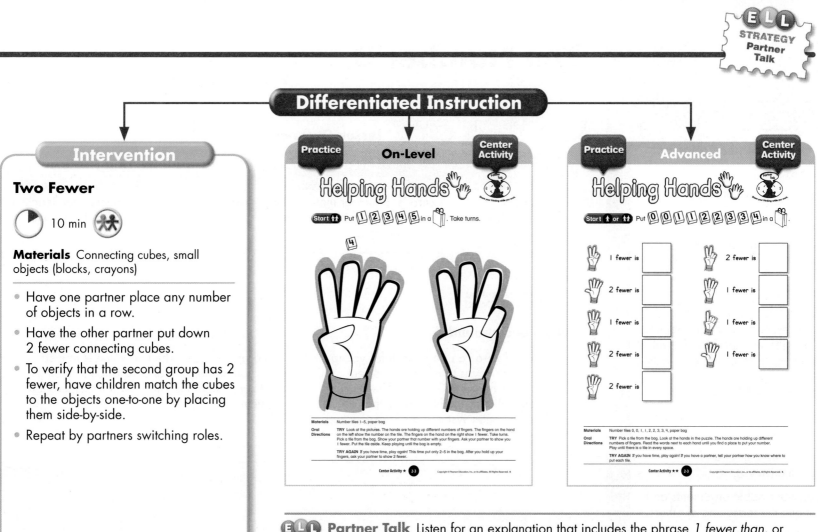

ELL Partner Talk Listen for an explanation that includes the phrase *1 fewer than*, or *2 fewer than*, as a child holds up the number of fingers shown on the activity page, and then holds up fewer fingers after seeing a clue in the puzzle.

Leveled Homework

Reteaching Master

Name _____

Reteaching 2-3

1 and 2 Fewer

Directions Have children: ★–❷ look at the top frame and show 1 or 2 fewer in the bottom frame by tracing circles; ❸ look at the top frame and draw 2 fewer in the bottom frame; ❹ look at the top frame and draw 1 fewer in the bottom frame. Then have children look at all 4 exercises and circle the groups that show 2 fewer.

Also available in print

Practice Master

Name _____

Practice 2-3

1 and 2 Fewer

Children color 3 balls.

Children color 3 shapes.

Children color 2 skateboards.

Directions Have children look at the shaded objects and: ★ color balls to show 2 fewer; ❷ color shapes to show 1 fewer; ❸ color skateboards to show 1 fewer.

Also available in print

Enrichment Master

Name _____

Enrichment 2-3

Moo! Oink! Baa!

❷ Which has fewer?

5

3

Directions Have children: ★ color all the cows brown, the piglets pink, and leave the sheep white; ❷ count the cows and sheep in the big picture, record the numbers on the lines, and then circle the number that shows fewer animals.

Also available in print

Domain
Counting and Cardinality

Cluster
Know number names and the count sequence

Standard
K.CC.3 Write numbers from 0 to 20. Represent a number of objects with a written numeral 0–20 (with 0 representing a count of no objects).

Mathematical Practices

✔ Make sense of problems and persevere in solving them.

✔ Reason abstractly and quantitatively.

○ Construct viable arguments and critique the reasoning of others.

○ Model with mathematics.

✔ Use appropriate tools strategically.

✔ Attend to precision.

○ Look for and make use of structure.

✔ Look for and express regularity in repeated reasoning.

The Number 0

 **Lesson Overview**

Objective	Essential Understanding	Vocabulary	Materials
Children will understand that *zero* means *none*.	Zero is a number that tells how many objects there are when there are none.	**zero** **none**	Counters (or Teaching Tool 32), crayons

PROFESSIONAL DEVELOPMENT

Math Background

The idea of zero can be difficult for young children. The key is to name the correct set, as in "1 nest, but 0 birds." The 0 is the foundational concept that makes the place-value numeration system possible by acting as a placeholder when no value is named. The comprehension of zero is foundational to future use of the Hindu-Arabic numeration system.

1 Daily Common Core Review

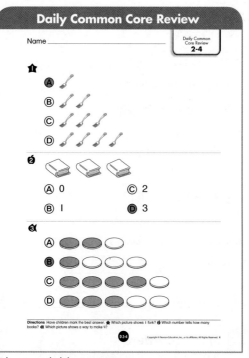

Also available in print

Content Reviewed

Exercise 1   Count Objects

Exercise 2   Use Numbers to Tell How Many

Exercise 3   Identify Ways to Make 4

⏳ 30 min **Problem-Based Interactive Learning**

Overview Children will recognize that a group can have no objects.

Focus What number would you use to show no objects, or none?

Materials Counters (or Teaching Tool 32), crayons

Vocabulary **zero**, **none**

 **Set the Purpose** Remind children that they have learned about the numbers 1 to 5. *You will learn about the number 0 in this lesson.*

Connect Draw groups of 1–5 stars on the board. As you point to each group, have children say the number that tells how many.

MATHEMATICAL PRACTICES

Make Sense of Problems
Ask children if a group can have no objects and if there is a number to represent this fact.

Pose the Problem *Anna is in her vegetable garden. She does not see any potatoes in the basket. The basket is empty. How can she use a number to show that the basket is empty?* Have children share their ideas before modeling the solution.

Academic Vocabulary Explain to children that when you use the word **zero**, you are talking about **none**. *If Anna had 3 carrots and no potatoes, what number would you use to show no potatoes?*

Model Write 0 on the board and say the word *zero* aloud. Have children repeat the word. *Anna can use this number to tell how many potatoes are in the basket. How many counters should we put on our workmats to show how many potatoes Anna saw in the basket?* [None] Direct children's attention to the first horizontal rectangle on the left. *How many boxes are shaded in?* [None, zero] *Should we color any boxes in for the number 0? Why?* [No, because Anna did not see any potatoes in the basket.] *Later Anna sees 1 potato. Place 1 counter on your workmat. Now place 1 counter on your mat. Say the number with me as you count the counter. Let's color 1 shaded box to show the number 1. Then Anna sees 2 potatoes.* Continue to model 2.

The Number 0 Name _____

Topic 2 • Lesson 4   twenty-nine 29

Using Math Manipulatives Make sure children use the correct number of counters for each number.

Small Group Interaction Have partners work together to complete the student page as you tell more stories about Anna. *Anna picked 2 peppers. Show 2 counters on your mat. How many boxes will you color in?* [2] Continue: *Anna picked 1 cabbage. Anna picked 0 cucumbers.*

 If you wanted to count from 0 to 5, what number would come after 0? [1]

💻 **eTools Counters**
www.pearsonsuccessnet.com

Visual Learning

How many balloons is Peeps the bird holding? [3] *How do you know?* [By counting or placing a cube or counter on each balloon]

How many balloons does Peeps the bird have now? [Peeps has 2 balloons.] *What number tells how many balloons there are?* [2] *How do you know?* [I can count them.]

1 Visual Learning

Set the Purpose Call children's attention to the **Visual Learning Bridge** at the top of the page. *In this lesson, you will learn that zero means none.*

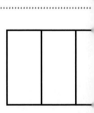 **Animated Glossary** Children can see highlighted words defined in the Online Student Edition.

zero, **none**

www.pearsonsuccessnet.com

2 Guided Practice

Remind children that *zero* can be used to tell that a group is empty.

Error Intervention

If children are not able to grasp that *zero* means *none*,

then help them understand this by showing a small clear plastic bag with 2 red cubes and a small plastic bag with no cubes. Hold up the bags, and help children compare them using the words *two* and *zero*.

Do you understand? *When there are no apples on the plate, how many cubes should you use to show none or nothing?* [Zero]

Reteaching Tell children to listen for the number in a sentence, such as, *Today I ate 2 sandwiches.* Ask children to show the number of sandwiches with color tiles. Repeat with other sentences using 0 to 5. When 0 comes up, ask children how they will show it and why.

1

2

3

Directions Have children count the pieces of fruit on each plate and then color the correct number of boxes to show many pieces of fruit.

Topic 2 • Lesson 4

How many balloons does Peeps the bird have now? [Peeps has 1 balloon.] What number tells how many balloons there are? [1]

How many balloons does Peeps the bird have now? [None] What number would you use to tell how many balloons Peeps has? [0]

Additional Activity

Hands Up for Zero

🕐 5 min 👥

- Play a game of *Hands Up for Zero* with the children.

- Say numbers from 0 to 5 in random order. Tell children to repeat the number and clap that many times. For zero, children should raise their hands in the air.

ions Have children count the flowers in each vase and then color the correct number of boxes to show how flowers.

thirty **30**

3 **Independent Practice**

Children count the flowers in each vase and then color in boxes to show each number.

30A

Close

Essential Understanding Zero is a number that tells how many objects there are when there are none. *Remember that you use zero to show none or nothing.*

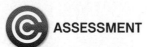

ASSESSMENT

Exercise 1 is worth 1 point.
Use the rubric to score Exercise 2.

Exercise 2

Reason Abstractly Children should be able to identify the plate with 0 apples.

ELL Use Repetition Repeat key words, phrases, and sentences before children begin their work.

Student Samples
3-point answer Children color in the correct plate and explain that *zero* means *none*.

2-point answer Children write a 0 on the middle plate.

1-point answer Children color in the wrong plate or all plates.

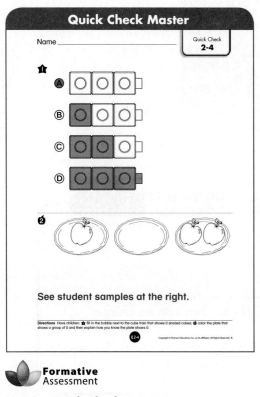

Quick Check Master

Name _____

Quick Check
2-4

Ⓐ ⃞⃞⃞

Ⓑ ⬛⃞⃞

Ⓒ ⬛⬛⃞

Ⓓ ⬛⬛⬛

② 🍎 ⬭ 🍎🍎

See student samples at the right.

Formative Assessment

Use the **Quick Check** to assess children's understanding.

Prescription for Differentiated Instruction
Use children's work on the **Quick Check** to prescribe differentiated instruction.

Points	Prescription
0–2	Intervention
3	On-Level
4	Advanced

Differentiated Instruction

Intervention

What's in the Cup?

🕐 10 min 🚶

Materials (per child) 5 connecting cubes, paper cup

- Have children count out 5 connecting cubes and place them in a paper cup.
- Remove 1 cube from the cup. Help children count the cubes that are still in the cup. Continue until there are no cubes in the cup.
- Guide children to understand that there are now 0 cubes in the cup; the cup is empty.

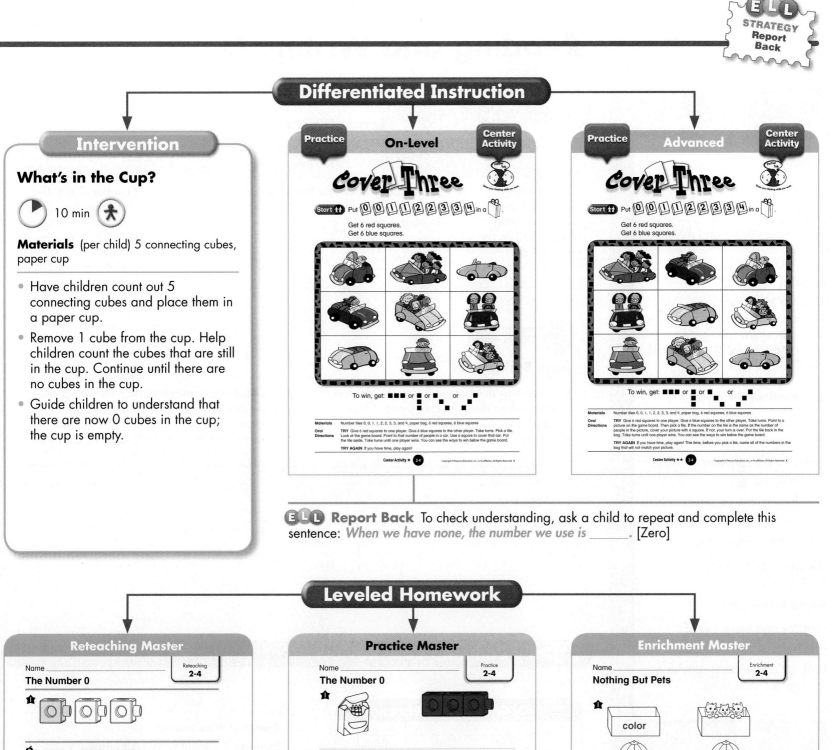

On-Level — Practice / Center Activity

Cover Three

Start ↟↟ Put 0 0 1 1 2 2 3 3 4 in a 📖

Get 6 red squares.
Get 6 blue squares.

To win, get: ■■■ or ▮ or ▮ or ▼

Materials Number tiles 0, 0, 1, 1, 2, 2, 3, 3, and 4, paper bag, 6 red squares, 6 blue squares
Oral Directions TRY Give 6 red squares to one player. Give 6 blue squares to the other player. Take turns. Pick a tile. Look at the game board. Point to that number of people in a car. Use a square to cover that car. Put the tile aside. Take turns until one player wins. You can see the ways to win below the game board.

TRY AGAIN If you have time, play again!

Center Activity ★ 2-4   Copyright © Pearson Education, Inc., or its affiliates. All Rights Reserved. K

Advanced — Practice / Center Activity

Cover Three

Start ↟↟ Put 0 0 1 1 2 2 3 3 4 in a 📖

Get 6 red squares.
Get 6 blue squares.

To win, get: ■■■ or ▮ or ▼

Materials Number tiles 0, 0, 1, 1, 2, 2, 3, 3, and 4, paper bag, 6 red squares, 6 blue squares
Oral Directions TRY Give 6 red squares to one player. Give 6 blue squares to the other player. Take turns. Point to a picture on the game board. Then pick a tile. If the number on the tile is the same as the number of people in the picture, cover your picture with a square. If not, your turn is over. Put the tile back in the bag. Take turns until one player wins. You can see the ways to win below the game board.

TRY AGAIN If you have time, play again! This time, before you pick a tile, name all of the numbers in the bag that will not match your picture.

Center Activity ★★ 2-4   Copyright © Pearson Education, Inc., or its affiliates. All Rights Reserved. K

E L L Report Back To check understanding, ask a child to repeat and complete this sentence: *When we have none, the number we use is _____.* [Zero]

Leveled Homework

Reteaching Master

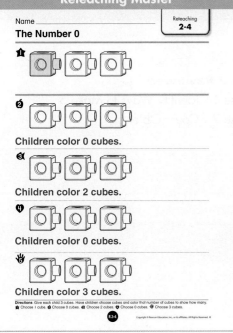

Name _____ Reteaching **2-4**

The Number 0

❶
❷ Children color 0 cubes.
❸ Children color 2 cubes.
❹ Children color 0 cubes.
✋ Children color 3 cubes.

Directions Give each child 3 cubes. Have children choose cubes and color that number of cubes to show how many. ★ Choose 1 cube. ❷ Choose 0 cubes. ❸ Choose 2 cubes. ❹ Choose 0 cubes. ✋ Choose 3 cubes.

R2-4   Copyright © Pearson Education, Inc., or its affiliates. All Rights Reserved. K

Also available in print

Practice Master

Name _____ Practice **2-4**

The Number 0

❶
❷
❸
❹

Directions Have children count the objects in each container and then color the correct number of cubes to show how many objects.

P2-4   Copyright © Pearson Education, Inc., or its affiliates. All Rights Reserved. K

Also available in print

Enrichment Master

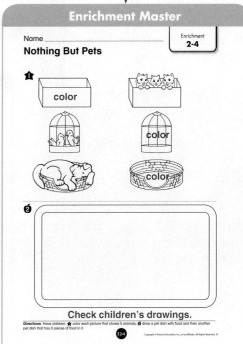

Name _____ Enrichment **2-4**

Nothing But Pets

❶ color / color / color / color
❷

Check children's drawings.

Directions Have children: ★ color each picture that shows 0 animals. ❷ draw a pet dish with food and then another pet dish that has 0 pieces of food in it.

E2-4   Copyright © Pearson Education, Inc., or its affiliates. All Rights Reserved. K

Also available in print

DIGITAL eTools **Counters**
www.pearsonsuccessnet.com

DIGITAL eTools **Counters**
www.pearsonsuccessnet.com

DIGITAL eTools **Counters**
www.pearsonsuccessnet.com

Domain

Counting and Cardinality

Cluster

Know number names and the count sequence

Standard

K.CC.3 Write numbers from 0 to 20. Represent a number of objects with a written numeral 0–20 (with 0 representing a count of no objects). Also **K.CC.4., K.CC.5**

Mathematical Practices

☑ Make sense of problems and persevere in solving them.

☑ Reason abstractly and quantitatively.

○ Construct viable arguments and critique the reasoning of others.

○ Model with mathematics.

☑ Use appropriate tools strategically.

○ Attend to precision.

○ Look for and make use of structure.

☑ Look for and express regularity in repeated reasoning.

Reading and Writing 0

 **Lesson Overview**

Objective	Essential Understanding	Vocabulary	Materials
Children will recognize and write the numeral that describes the quantity of 0.	Zero is a number that tells how many objects there are when there are none.		Number Cards 0–5 (Teaching Tool 5), counters (or Teaching Tool 32), Writing Practice 4, 5, 0 (Teaching Tool 13)

Ⓒ **PROFESSIONAL DEVELOPMENT**

Math Background

Representing numbers in a variety of ways helps children gain number sense. Often children will understand one representation of a number, such as a numeral, but not a physical representation, such as with place-value blocks. Understanding that there are multiple representations of a number will help children later on with their algebraic thinking.

1 **Daily Common Core Review**

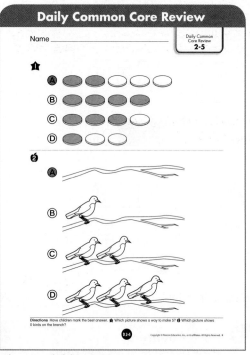

Content Reviewed

Exercise 1   Identify Ways to Make 5

Exercise 2   Count Objects

Also available in print

 30 min # Problem-Based Interactive Learning

Overview Children will read and write the number 0.

Focus What number would you use to show no objects, or none?

Materials Number Cards 0–5 (Teaching Tool 5), counters (or Teaching Tool 32)

Set the Purpose Remind children that they have learned how to read and write numbers 1 to 5. *You will learn how to read and write the symbol for the number 0 in this lesson.*

Connect Display the number cards for 1–5 in order along the ledge of the board. Point to each number and have children identify it.

MATHEMATICAL
PRACTICES

Reason Quantitatively
Ask children how they would represent no objects, or none.

Pose the Problem *James is in kindergarten class. He doesn't see any pencils. How can he use a number to show no pencils, or none?* Have children share their ideas before modeling the solution.

Model *James sees 2 crayons in the classroom. Move that many counters onto your workmat. Let's count the counters together.* [1, 2] *Then James sees 1 eraser.* Continue to model 1. Then remind children that James doesn't see any pencils. Hold up the number card for 0 and say the word *zero* aloud. Have children repeat the word. *James can use this number to show how many pencils he sees in the classroom. Say the number with me.* [Zero] *How many counters should I place on my mat?* [None] *Zero means none. Let's try writing the number 0 in the air.* Hold up the number card for 0 again and trace over the number as children watch. Then skywrite the number 0 with children. *Now let's trace the number 0 on your page.* Remind children to start at the dot. Have children trace the 0s on the left side of the student page.

Peer Questioning Have partners work together to show the correct number of counters on the student page and then practice writing the number 0 on the right side of the page. Guide children to start writing 0 at the dot. As they write, have children ask each other questions about what they are doing such as: "How many counters did you show for 0?" and "What number will you write?"

 Play a game of *I Spy* with children. Have children look around the classroom to find the numerals 0 to 5.

DIGITAL eTools **Counters**
www.pearsonsuccessnet.com

Visual Learning

How many pencils are in the holder? [1] *What number would you write to show how many pencils there are?* [1]

How many pencils are in the pencil holder now? [None]

1 Visual Learning

Set the Purpose Call attention to the **Visual Learning Bridge** at the top of the page. *In this lesson, you will learn how to read and write 0.*

2 Guided Practice

Remind children that there is a special symbol for the number 0.

Error Intervention

If children have difficulty writing the numbers,

then have children practice by using a finger to trace over the numbers on number cards (Teaching Tool 5), or they can practice writing 0 on Teaching Tool 13.

Do you understand? *When the pencil holder is empty, what number would you write to show how many?* [0]

Reteaching Have children practice making zeros by providing them with beans, paint, or bits of paper. They can glue or paint their zeros onto a sheet of construction paper.

Directions Have children count the pencils in each pencil holder and then practice writing the matching numbers, beginning at each black dot.

Topic 2 • Lesson 5

What do you think this number will be if you trace it? [0] Where do you start to trace the number? [At the dot] Trace the number.

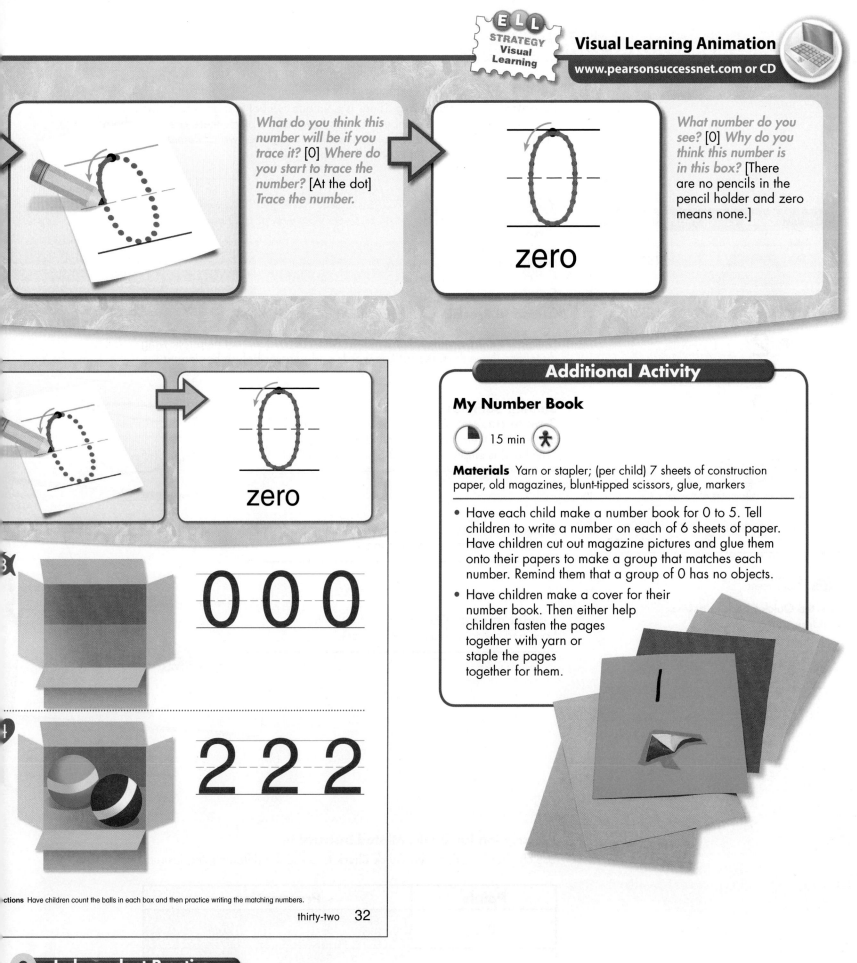

zero

What number do you see? [0] Why do you think this number is in this box? [There are no pencils in the pencil holder and zero means none.]

zero

0 0 0

2 2 2

...ctions Have children count the balls in each box and then practice writing the matching numbers.

thirty-two   32

Additional Activity

My Number Book

⏱ 15 min   👤

Materials Yarn or stapler; (per child) 7 sheets of construction paper, old magazines, blunt-tipped scissors, glue, markers

• Have each child make a number book for 0 to 5. Tell children to write a number on each of 6 sheets of paper. Have children cut out magazine pictures and glue them onto their papers to make a group that matches each number. Remind them that a group of 0 has no objects.

• Have children make a cover for their number book. Then either help children fasten the pages together with yarn or staple the pages together for them.

3   Independent Practice

Children count the objects in each box and then write the number that tells how many there are in each group.

32A

Close

Essential Understanding There is a unique symbol that goes with each number word. Zero is a number that tells how many objects there are when there are none. *There is a symbol that goes with each number word. Remember that we use the number zero to show none or nothing.*

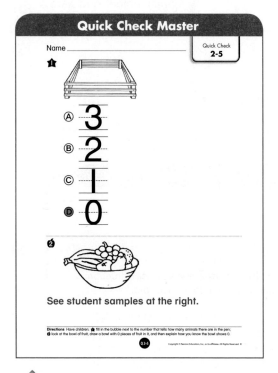

Quick Check Master

Name _____

Quick Check
2-5

①

Ⓐ 3
Ⓑ 2
Ⓒ 1
Ⓓ 0

②

See student samples at the right.

Directions Have children: ① fill in the bubble next to the number that tells how many animals there are in the pen; ② look at the bowl of fruit, draw a bowl with 0 pieces of fruit in it, and then explain how you know the bowl shows 0.

2-5

Copyright © Pearson Education, Inc., or its affiliates. All Rights Reserved.

Formative Assessment

Use the **Quick Check** to assess children's understanding.

Ⓒ **ASSESSMENT**

Exercise 1 is worth 1 point.
Use the rubric to score Exercise 2.

Exercise 2

Attend to Precision Children should be able to write 0.

E L L Use Repetition For children who need additional help following directions, have them repeat key words and phrases before beginning their work.

Student Samples
3-point answer Children draw an empty bowl and explain their answers. A child might say, "The bowl is empty so it has 0 pieces of fruit."

2-point answer Children draw an empty bowl but do not provide an explanation.

1-point answer Children draw fruit in the bowl and do not explain their answers.

Prescription for Differentiated Instruction
Use children's work on the **Quick Check** to prescribe differentiated instruction.

Points	Prescription
0–2	Intervention
3	On-Level
4	Advanced

Differentiated Instruction

Intervention

Zero Blocks

🕐 10 min 🧍

Materials (per child) Number Cards 0–5 (Teaching Tool 5), 5 blocks, basket

- Place 5 blocks in the basket and have the child count them. Put the card for 5 next to the basket.
- Remove 1 block and have the child count blocks. Put the card for 4 next to the basket. Repeat for 3, 2, and 1.
- Remove the last block. Guide the child to say that there are no blocks in the basket. Show the 0 card and explain that 0 stands for no objects.

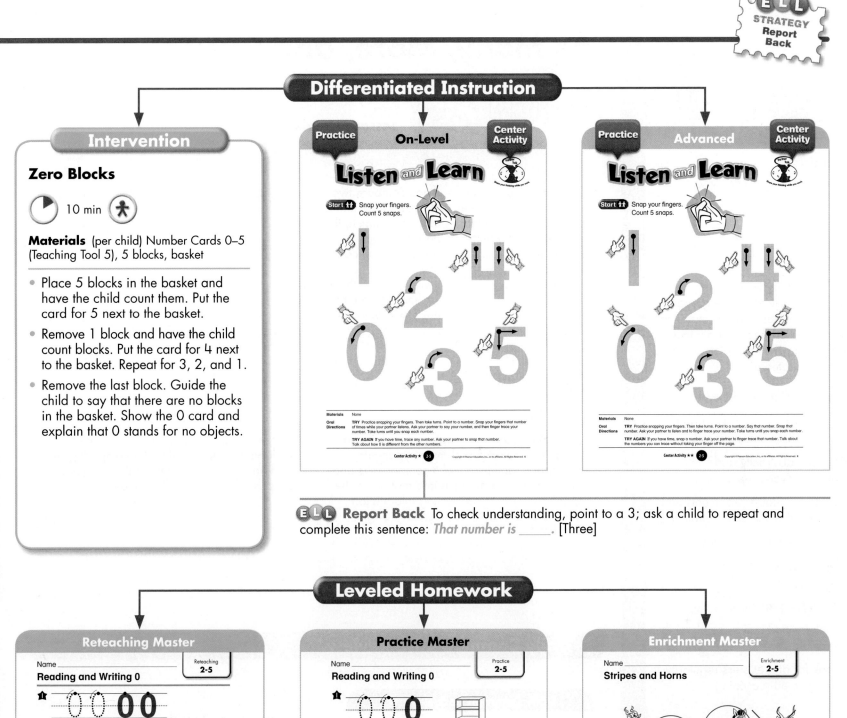

On-Level — Practice / Center Activity

Listen and Learn

Start ↑↑ Snap your fingers. Count 5 snaps.

Advanced — Practice / Center Activity

Listen and Learn

Start ↑↑ Snap your fingers. Count 5 snaps.

ELL Report Back To check understanding, point to a 3; ask a child to repeat and complete this sentence: *That number is _____.* [Three]

Leveled Homework

Reteaching Master

Name _____
Reading and Writing 0
Reteaching 2-5

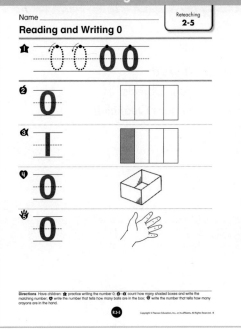

Also available in print

Practice Master

Name _____
Reading and Writing 0
Practice 2-5

Also available in print

Enrichment Master

Name _____
Stripes and Horns
Enrichment 2-5

2 animals have 0 horns and 0 stripes.

Also available in print

DIGITAL eTools **Counters**
www.pearsonsuccessnet.com

DIGITAL MindPoint Quiz Show
Numbers 0 to 5
www.pearsonsuccessnet.com

DIGITAL eTools **Counters**
www.pearsonsuccessnet.com

As Many, More, and Fewer

Common Core

Domain
Counting and Cardinality

Cluster
Comparing numbers.

Standard
K.CC.6 Identify whether the number of objects in one group is greater than, less than, or equal to the number of objects in another group, e.g., by using matching and counting strategies.

Mathematical Practices

☑ Make sense of problems and persevere in solving them.

☑ Reason abstractly and quantitatively.

○ Construct viable arguments and critique the reasoning of others.

○ Model with mathematics.

☑ Use appropriate tools strategically.

☑ Attend to precision.

○ Look for and make use of structure.

☑ Look for and express regularity in repeated reasoning.

Quick and Easy Lesson Overview

Objective	Essential Understanding	Vocabulary	Materials
Children will use one-to-one correspondence to compare two groups and determine whether one group has more, fewer, or as many as the other group.	If you compare two groups of objects and the number of objects match, the groups have the same number of objects. If you compare two groups and one group has items left over, that group has more. The other group has fewer objects.	**as many**	Connecting cubes, crayon

© PROFESSIONAL DEVELOPMENT

Math Background

Research says ... graph comprehension is based on knowledge of the components of a graph, ability to make comparisons and do computations from the information on the graph, and facility in relating information back to its context (Friel, Curcio & Bright, 2001).

This lesson begins a section in which children build their graphing skills by comparing sets of data to read and create different types of graphs related to familiar situations.

1 Daily Common Core Review

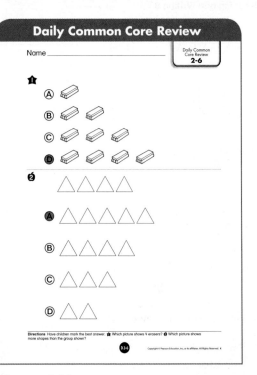

Content Reviewed

Exercise 1 Count Objects

Exercise 2 Compare Quantities

Also available in print

 30 min # Problem-Based Interactive Learning

Overview Children will use one-to-one correspondence to compare two groups and determine which group has more, fewer, or as many as the other group.

Focus How does matching objects in two groups of objects help you know which group has more, fewer, or as many as the other group?

Materials Connecting cubes, crayon

Vocabulary as many

Set the Purpose Remind children that they learned to compare two groups of objects to determine which number is greater and which is less. *Now you will learn about another way to compare groups of objects and answer questions about them.*

Connect Provide different-colored connecting cubes for children to sort.

MATHEMATICAL PRACTICES

Reason Abstractly
Ask children how they can use one-to-one correspondence to compare two groups to determine which group has more, fewer, or as many as the other group.

Academic Vocabulary Explain that when two groups have the same, or equal, number of objects, one group has **as many** as the other group.

Pose the Problem *Mrs. Riley made two rows of cubes. How can you find out which row has more cubes?* Have children share ideas.

Model Put 2 cubes in a row in the center of the workmat and have children do the same. *Let's color in the first ten-frame to show these two cubes.* Have children color over the shaded squares in the top row. Place 3 cubes in a row below the other row and have children do the same. Have children color over the shaded squares in the bottom row. On the workmat, show children how to push each cube in the top row down to match a cube in the bottom row. *The row with a cube left over has more. Which row has more cubes?* [The bottom row] Continue by making a row of 3 cubes and a row of 4 cubes, then coloring the middle frame to match. *Which row has fewer?* [The top row] Children repeat with 4 cubes in each row in the bottom frame.

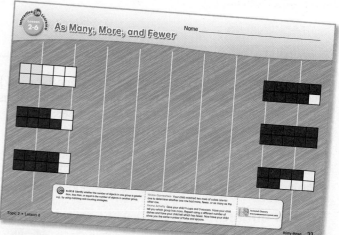

Use Math Manipulatives After children have matched cubes, have them touch the row (or rows) of cubes that answers each question.

Small Group Interaction Have children complete the right side of the page as you dictate the cubes for each row: Top frame: 5 cubes in top row, 4 cubes in bottom row. Middle frame: 5 cubes in each row. Bottom frame: 4 cubes in top row, 2 cubes in bottom row. Refer to the graphs and ask questions such as: *Which row has more? Which row has fewer cubes? Which graph shows the same number?*

Have partners take turns making two rows of cubes and asking questions about the rows. Ask them to use the words *more, fewer,* and *as many as* in their questions.

eTools **Counters**
www.pearsonsuccessnet.com

Visual Learning

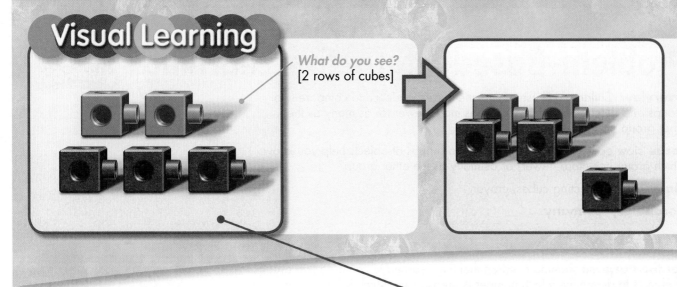

What do you see? [2 rows of cubes]

What can you tell when the cubes are matched one to one? [Whether one row has more cubes, fewer cubes, or as many cubes as the other row] *Does one row have more cubes than the other?* [Yes] *Which row has more?* [The bottom row; the row with red cubes]

1 Visual Learning

Set the Purpose Call children's attention to the **Visual Learning Bridge** at the top of the page. *In this lesson, you will learn about comparing groups of objects to find out whether one group has more, fewer, or as many as the other group.*

 Animated Glossary Children can use highlighted words defined in the Online Student Edition.

as many

www.pearsonsuccessnet.com

2 Guided Practice

Remind children that they can match objects one-to-one to figure out whether one group has more, fewer, or as many objects as another group. The suggestions below apply to Exercises 1–6.

Error Intervention

If children have difficulties matching objects one-to-one,

then have them draw lines from one object to the other.

Do you understand? *How can you find out whether one group of objects has more, fewer, or as many as the other group?* [I can use objects to show each group. Then I can match the objects one-to-one. The group with an object or objects left over has more. The other group has fewer. If each object has a match, there are as many in one group as the other.]

Reteaching Show children a row of 4 marking pens without tops and a row of 3 marking-pen tops below the pens. *When we compare groups, we match them one-to-one.* Have children match the pens and tops. Then have them point to the row that has more and the row that has fewer. Continue with other comparisons.

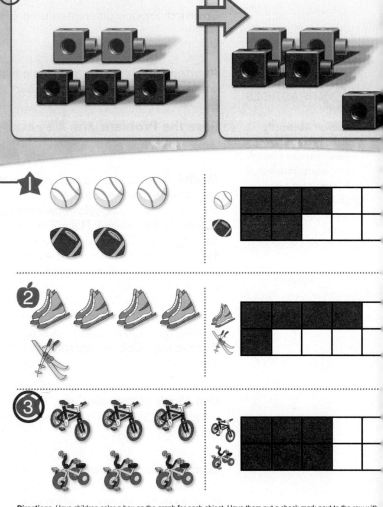

Directions Have children color a box on the graph for each object. Have them put a check mark next to the row with more objects. If the number of objects is the same, children should circle the exercise number.

Topic 2 • Lesson 6

E L L
STRATEGY
Visual
Learning

Visual Learning Animation

www.pearsonsuccessnet.com or CD

Thomas colored in some boxes. What does his coloring show? [The cubes he put in each row]

Why is the bottom row of boxes checked? [It's the row that has more.]

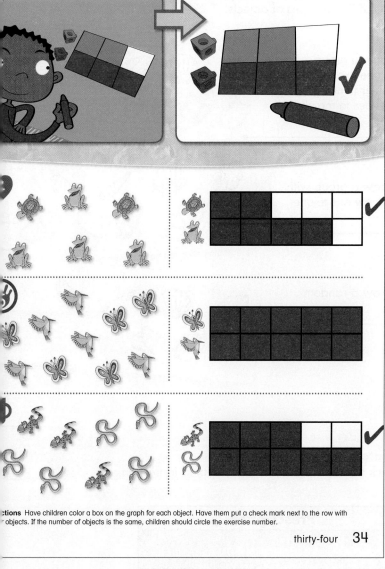

Directions Have children color a box on the graph for each object. Have them put a check mark next to the row with ~~fewer~~ objects. If the number of objects is the same, children should circle the exercise number.

Additional Activity

Pour More or Fewer

⏰ 10–15 min 👥

Materials (per pair) 10 two-color counters (or Teaching Tool 32), 2 small cups, yarn loop

- Each child puts some counters in a cup and pours them onto the table.
- Partners line up their counters in rows and show one-to-one correspondence.
- Call out *more* or *fewer*. Children take turns putting a yarn loop around the row that shows what you call.

3 **Independent Practice**

Children color a box on the graph for each object. Then they put a check mark next to the row with fewer objects or they circle the exercise number if there is the same number of objects.

34A

Close

Essential Understanding If you compare two groups of objects and the number of objects match, the groups have the same number of objects. If you compare two groups and one group has items left over, that group has more. The other group has fewer objects. *Matching the objects in two rows helps you know whether one group has more, fewer, or as many as the other group.*

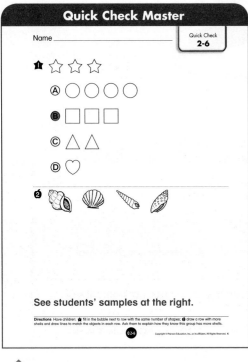

Quick Check Master

Name _____ Quick Check **2-6**

See students' samples at the right.

Formative Assessment

Use the **Quick Check** to assess children's understanding.

ASSESSMENT

Exercise 1 is worth 1 point.
Use the rubric to score Exercise 2.

Exercise 2
Use Appropriate Tools Children should be able to draw a group of items with more.

ELL **Use Repetition** If children need additional help, make comparisons during the day with different types of objects.

Student Samples
3-point answer Children draw a group with more, draw lines to show one-to-one correspondence, and explain their thinking: A child might say," I can draw lines to match. My row has shells that are left over."

2-point answer Children draw a group with more but do not draw lines to show one-to-one correspondence.

1-point answer Children draw a random number of shells.

Prescription for Differentiated Instruction
Use children's work on the **Quick Check** to prescribe differentiated instruction.

Points	Prescription
0–2	Intervention
3	On-Level
4	Advanced

Differentiated Instruction

Intervention

Echo, Echo

🕐 5 min 👥

- Make a row with 4 children and a row with 2 children. Have them stand facing each other.
- Have the first child in the 4-child row call "echo" to her/his partner. Have the partner answer back.
- Continue until each child has called out.
- Ask: *Why didn't some children get their call returned?* [Because there are more children in one row.] Ask children what they could change so that each child gets an "echo." Then add 2 children to the row with fewer children so that one row has as many as the other.

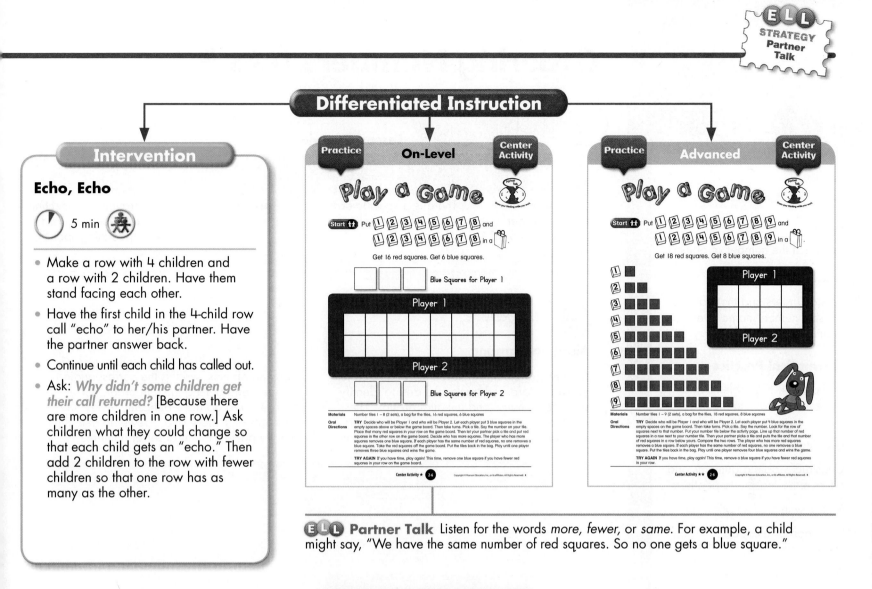

ELL Partner Talk Listen for the words *more, fewer,* or *same*. For example, a child might say, "We have the same number of red squares. So no one gets a blue square."

Leveled Homework

Reteaching Master

Name _____
As Many, More, and Fewer Reteaching 2-6

Also available in print

Practice Master

Name _____
As Many, More, and Fewer Practice 2-6

Also available in print

Enrichment Master

Name _____
On the Ball Enrichment 2-6

② Check that children have drawn more than 3 balls.

③ Check that children have drawn fewer than 4 balls.

Also available in print

DIGITAL eTools **Counters** www.pearsonsuccessnet.com

DIGITAL eTools **Counters** www.pearsonsuccessnet.com

DIGITAL eTools **Counters** www.pearsonsuccessnet.com

Ordering Numbers 0 to 5

 **Lesson Overview**

Objective	Essential Understanding	Vocabulary	Materials
Children will use objects to order numbers 0 to 5 in sequence.	There is a specific order to the set of whole numbers.	**order**	12 crayons, connecting cubes, Number Cards 0–5 (Teaching Tool 5), glue

Ⓒ PROFESSIONAL DEVELOPMENT

Math Background

In previous lessons, children have learned to count forward and backward and to identify and create equal and unequal groups. These concepts prepare children to order numbers. In most cases, children will not have problems drawing objects, writing the corresponding number, and putting them in order. For children who do have difficulty, review the concepts of *1 more* and *1 fewer* to help them see the pattern in the order of numbers.

1 Daily Common Core Review

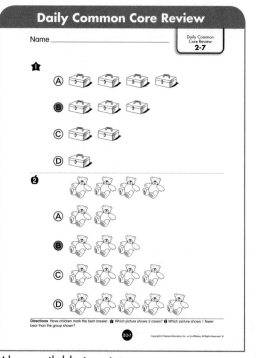

Content Reviewed

Exercise 1   Count Objects

Exercise 2   Identify 1 Fewer

Also available in print

 30 min **Problem-Based Interactive Learning**

Overview Children will use objects to order numbers from 0 to 5 in sequence.

Focus How can you use objects to show the number sequence 0 to 5?

Materials 12 crayons; (per child) connecting cubes, Number Cards 0–5 (Teaching Tool 5), glue

Vocabulary order

Set the Purpose Remind children that they have learned about the numbers 0 to 5. *You will learn the correct order for those numbers in this lesson.*

Connect Show 5 crayons on a table. *Who can make a group of crayons with 1 fewer crayon? Who can make a group with 2 fewer crayons?*

MATHEMATICAL
PRACTICES

Reason Quantitatively
Ask children how they would represent the numbers 0 to 5 with objects.

Academic Vocabulary *When you write numbers in the correct sequence, you can use the word* order *to tell about the numbers.*

Pose the Problem *Evan wants to use cubes to show the numbers 0 to 5 in the correct order. How can he do this?* Have children share their ideas.

Model Display the number cards in the correct order and have children say each number aloud as you point to it in sequence. Move 1 red cube onto the mat as children do the same. *How many cubes are there?* [1 cube] *Which number card tells how many?* Call on a volunteer to find the number 1 card. Stack 2 red cubes onto the workmat. Have children stack 2 red cubes and move the "tower" onto their workmats. *How many cubes are there in this tower?* [2 cubes] *Which number card tells how many?* Call on a volunteer to find the number 2 card. Continue with each number. *How many cubes should we show for the number 0?* [None] Display the stacks in sequential order and help children note the pattern of one more. Make sure children stack their cubes and line their towers up next to the appropriate number cards to make a staircase pattern. Point out that each tower has 1 more cube than the tower before it if they count from 0 to 5.

Peer Questioning Have children cut out the number cards from Teaching Tool 5 and then glue each number in correct order in the boxes on the workmat. Have partners work together and ask each other questions.

How does the pattern change if you put your towers in order from 5 to 0? [Each tower has 1 fewer cube than the tower before it.]

eTools **Counters**
www.pearsonsuccessnet.com

Visual Learning

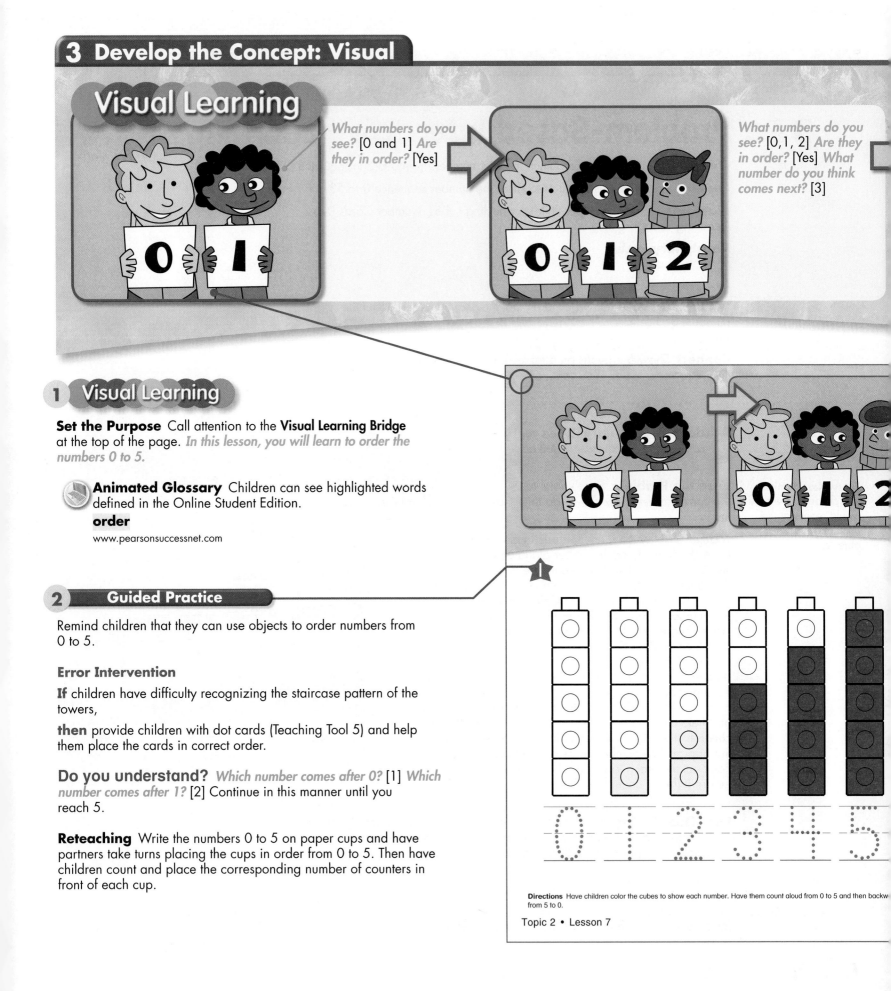

What numbers do you see? [0 and 1] *Are they in order?* [Yes]

What numbers do you see? [0,1, 2] *Are they in order?* [Yes] *What number do you think comes next?* [3]

1 Visual Learning

Set the Purpose Call attention to the **Visual Learning Bridge** at the top of the page. *In this lesson, you will learn to order the numbers 0 to 5.*

Animated Glossary Children can see highlighted words defined in the Online Student Edition.

order

www.pearsonsuccessnet.com

2 Guided Practice

Remind children that they can use objects to order numbers from 0 to 5.

Error Intervention

If children have difficulty recognizing the staircase pattern of the towers,

then provide children with dot cards (Teaching Tool 5) and help them place the cards in correct order.

Do you understand? *Which number comes after 0?* [1] *Which number comes after 1?* [2] Continue in this manner until you reach 5.

Reteaching Write the numbers 0 to 5 on paper cups and have partners take turns placing the cups in order from 0 to 5. Then have children count and place the corresponding number of counters in front of each cup.

Directions Have children color the cubes to show each number. Have them count aloud from 0 to 5 and then backw from 5 to 0.

Topic 2 • Lesson 7

What numbers do you see? [0, 1, 2, 3, 4, 5] *How do you know they are in order?* [Because each number is one more than the one before it] *Which number is to the left of 1?* [0]

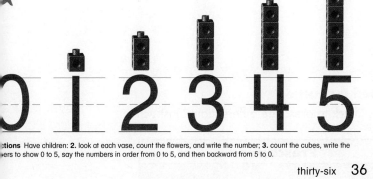

Additional Activity

Number Puzzles

🕐 15 min 👥

Materials (per pair) Number Cards 1–5 (Teaching Tool 5), blunt-tipped scissors

- Tell children to cut the number 2 card into 2 pieces, the number 3 card into 3 pieces, and so on.
- Have them mix up the pieces and reassemble the puzzles.
- Have children put the puzzles in order from 1 to 5. Then have them point to each number as they count forward from 1 to 5 and backward from 5 to 1.

ctions Have children: **2.** look at each vase, count the flowers, and write the number; **3.** count the cubes, write the ...ers to show 0 to 5, say the numbers in order from 0 to 5, and then backward from 5 to 0.

thirty-six **36**

3 Independent Practice

Children write numbers in order from 0 to 5.

Close

Essential Understanding There is a specific order to the set of whole numbers. *Numbers go in a certain order.*

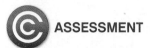 **ASSESSMENT**

Exercise 1 is worth 1 point.
Use the rubric to score Exercise 2.

Exercise 2

Use Appropriate Tools Children should be able to color cubes to represent each number.

ELL Use Repetition For children who need additional help following directions, have them repeat key words and phrases before beginning their work.

Student Samples
3-point answer Children color the cubes correctly to show each number and count aloud in order.

2-point answer Children color 4 out of 6 cube trains correctly.

1-point answer Children color 1 to 3 cube trains correctly.

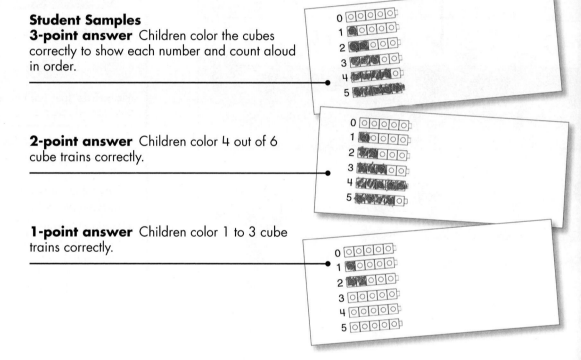

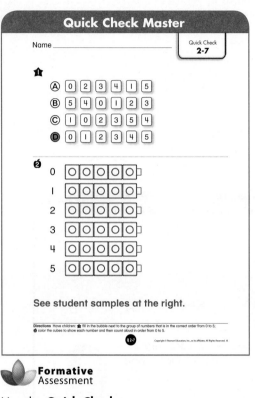

Formative Assessment

Use the **Quick Check** to assess children's understanding.

Prescription for Differentiated Instruction
Use children's work on the **Quick Check** to prescribe differentiated instruction.

Points	Prescription
0–2	Intervention
3	On-Level
4	Advanced

Differentiated Instruction

Intervention

Counting Jumps

🕐 10 min 👥

Materials 6 construction paper "lily pads" numbered 0–5, masking tape

- Tape the "lily pads" in order on a path across the floor.
- Tell children to pretend to be frogs jumping across a pond.
- As they jump on each "lily pad," have them say the number and make that many "ribbit" sounds.

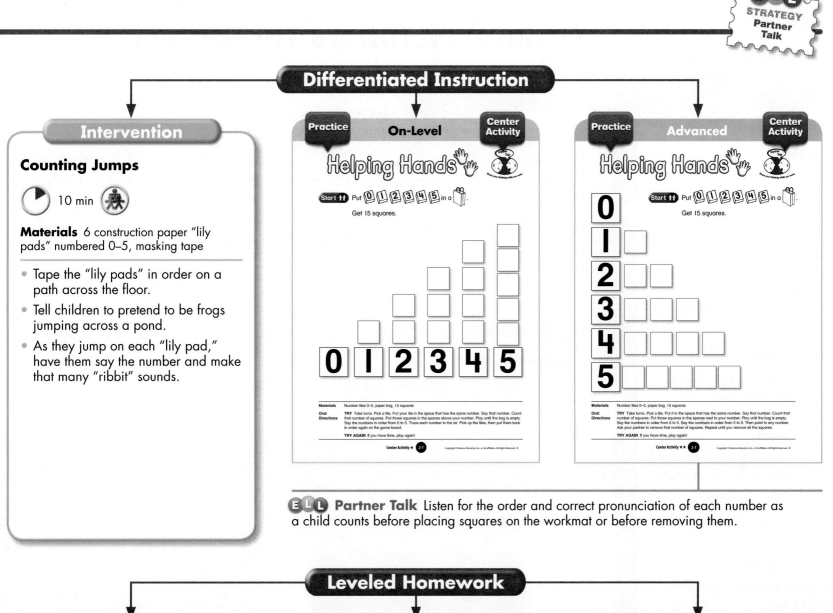

Practice | **On-Level** | **Center Activity**

Helping Hands

Start ↑↑ Put 0 1 2 3 4 5 in a bag.
Get 15 squares.

0 1 2 3 4 5

Materials Number tiles 0–5, paper bag, 15 squares
Oral Directions TRY Take turns. Pick a tile. Put your tile in the space that has the same number. Say that number. Count that number of squares. Put those squares in the spaces above your number. Play until the bag is empty. Say the numbers in order from 0 to 5. Trace each number in the air. Pick up the tiles, then put them back in order again on the game board.

TRY AGAIN If you have time, play again!

Center Activity ★ 2-7

Practice | **Advanced** | **Center Activity**

Helping Hands

Start ↑↑ Put 0 1 2 3 4 5 in a bag.
Get 15 squares.

0
1
2
3
4
5

Materials Number tiles 0–5, paper bag, 15 squares
Oral Directions TRY Take turns. Pick a tile. Put it in the space that has the same number. Say that number. Count that number of squares. Put those squares in the spaces next to your number. Play until the bag is empty. Say the numbers in order from 0 to 5. Say the numbers in order from 5 to 0. Then point to any number. Ask your partner to remove that number of squares. Repeat until you remove all the squares.

TRY AGAIN If you have time, play again!

Center Activity ★★ 2-7

ELL Partner Talk Listen for the order and correct pronunciation of each number as a child counts before placing squares on the workmat or before removing them.

Leveled Homework

Reteaching Master

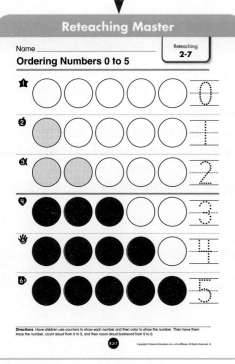

Name ____
Reteaching **2-7**
Ordering Numbers 0 to 5

Directions Have children use counters to show each number and then color to show the number. Then have them trace the number, count aloud from 0 to 5, and then count aloud backward from 5 to 0.
R 2-7

Also available in print

Practice Master

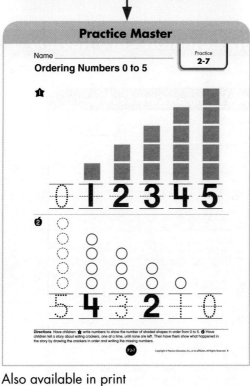

Name ____
Practice **2-7**
Ordering Numbers 0 to 5

Directions Have children: ① write numbers to show the number of shaded shapes in order from 0 to 5. ② Have children tell a story about eating crackers, one at a time, until none are left. Then have them show what happened in the story by drawing the crackers in order and writing the missing numbers.
P 2-7

Also available in print

Enrichment Master

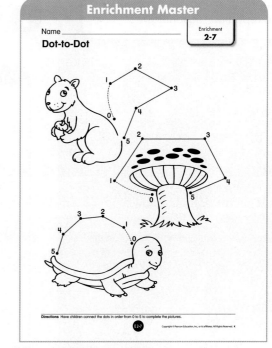

Name ____
Enrichment **2-7**
Dot-to-Dot

Directions Have children connect the dots in order from 0 to 5 to complete the pictures.
E 2-7

Also available in print

DIGITAL eTools **Counters** www.pearsonsuccessnet.com

DIGITAL eTools **Counters** www.pearsonsuccessnet.com

DIGITAL eTools **Counters** www.pearsonsuccessnet.com

Ordinal Numbers Through Fifth

Common Core

Domain
Counting and Cardinality

Cluster
Count to tell the number of objects.

Standard
K.CC.4 Understand the relationship between numbers and quantities; connect counting to cardinality. Also **K.CC.4.c**

Mathematical Practices

☑ Make sense of problems and persevere in solving them.

☑ Reason abstractly and quantitatively.

○ Construct viable arguments and critique the reasoning of others.

○ Model with mathematics.

☑ Use appropriate tools strategically.

☑ Attend to precision.

○ Look for and make use of structure.

☑ Look for and express regularity in repeated reasoning.

 **Lesson Overview**

Objective	Essential Understanding	Vocabulary	Materials
Children will use words *first* through *fifth* to identify ordinal positions.	Numbers can be used to tell order (ordinal numbers). Positions/order in a row can be found by counting, and ordinal names are similar to number names.	**first** **second** **third** **fourth** **fifth**	Number Cards 1–5, (Teaching Tool 5), blunt-tipped scissors, glue

PROFESSIONAL DEVELOPMENT

Math Background

Children need more practice with ordinal numbers to avoid name confusion between numerals and ordinal numbers.

1 Daily Common Core Review

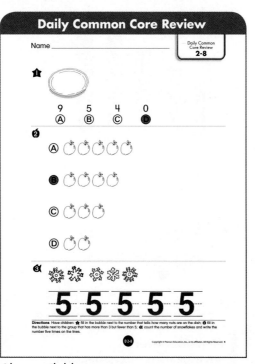

Also available in print

Content Reviewed

Exercise 1 Use Numbers to Tell How Many

Exercise 2 Use Language such as *1 More Than* and *1 Fewer Than*

Exercise 3 Write Numbers

30 min Problem-Based Interactive Learning

Hands-On Minds-On

Overview Children will identify which object in a row of five objects is in a given ordinal position by naming its color.

Focus How can you describe the order of five things in a row?

Materials Number Cards 1–5 (Teaching Tool 5), glue, blunt-tipped scissors

Vocabulary first, second, third, fourth, fifth

Set the Purpose Remind children that they learned how to use numbers to tell how many. *Now you will learn other types of words that tell about order.*

Connect Call five children to the front of the classroom. Give each child a number card from 1 to 5 in random order. Have children put themselves in number order.

MATHEMATICAL PRACTICES

Reason Abstractly
Ask children how numbers can tell how many, and can also tell order.

Pose the Problem *Tusk sees five ladybugs in a row on a leaf. Each ladybug is a different color. How can we find each ladybug's place in the row?* Have children share their ideas. *Which ladybug do you think is fourth? Talk to your partner and try to decide.*

Academic Vocabulary Point out to children that **first**, **second**, **third**, **fourth**, and **fifth** are words that tell the order of things in a row or line. *Demonstrate by asking five children to stand in a row. Point to each child as you say first, second, third, and so on, in order. Then repeat, and have children echo you.*

Model Have children cut out the pictures of ladybugs. *How many ladybugs do we have?* Explain that they will glue the ladybugs in the boxes on the workmat by following your instructions. *Glue the orange ladybug in the first box. Glue the yellow ladybug in the second box. Glue the red ladybug in the third box. Which ladybug should we glue in the fourth box?* Decide with children. *Which color ladybug should we glue in the fifth box? We use the numbers 1, 2, 3, 4, 5 to count five things. We use the words first, second, third, fourth, fifth to tell the place of each thing.* Continue in the same way, reinforcing the ordinal numbers by asking children to name the colors of the ladybugs in order.

Peer Questioning Encourage partners to take turns asking questions about the ladybugs on their workmats using the ordinal words *first* through *fifth*. *What color is the fifth ladybug? How do you know that the second ladybug is yellow?*

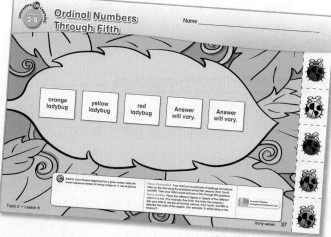

Sample answers shown.

Extend *What color is the ladybug just before the fifth ladybug? What color is the ladybug just after the second ladybug?* [Red]

DIGITAL eTools **Counters** www.pearsonsuccessnet.com

Visual Learning

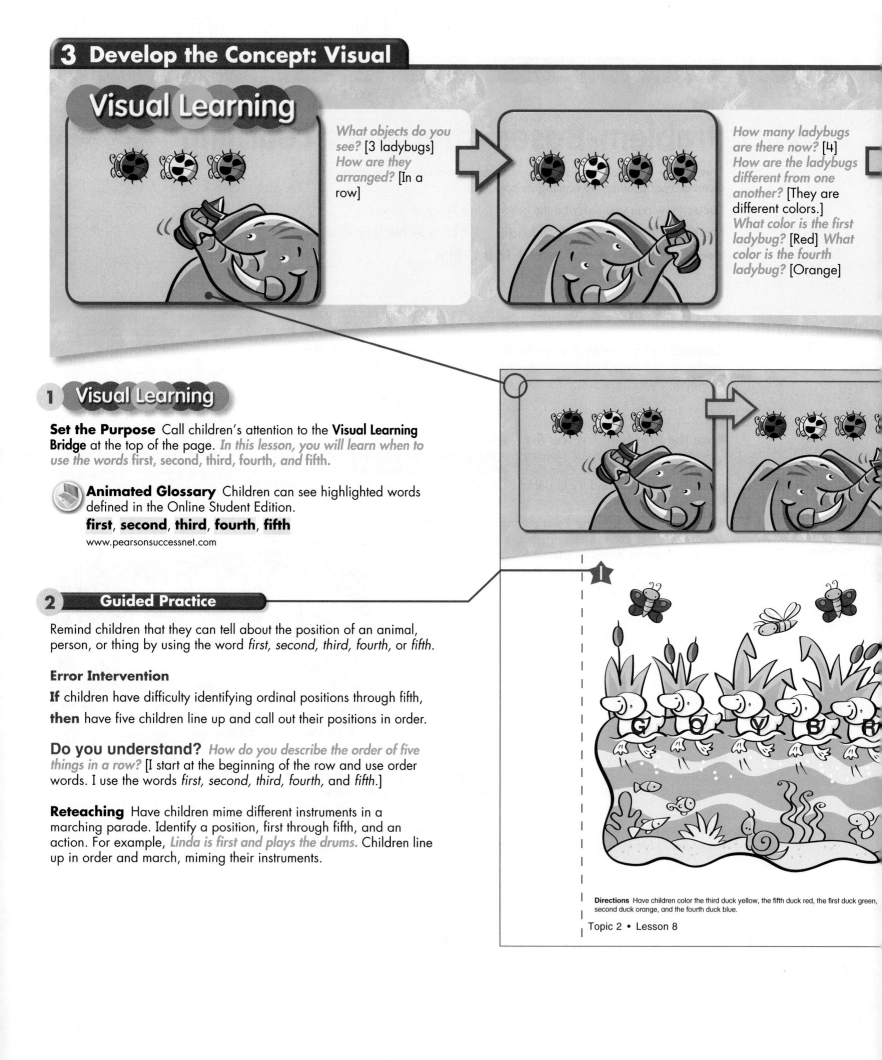

What objects do you see? [3 ladybugs]
How are they arranged? [In a row]

How many ladybugs are there now? [4]
How are the ladybugs different from one another? [They are different colors.]
What color is the first ladybug? [Red] *What color is the fourth ladybug?* [Orange]

1 Visual Learning

Set the Purpose Call children's attention to the **Visual Learning Bridge** at the top of the page. *In this lesson, you will learn when to use the words* first, second, third, fourth, *and* fifth.

Animated Glossary Children can see highlighted words defined in the Online Student Edition.
first, **second**, **third**, **fourth**, **fifth**
www.pearsonsuccessnet.com

2 Guided Practice

Remind children that they can tell about the position of an animal, person, or thing by using the word *first, second, third, fourth,* or *fifth.*

Error Intervention

If children have difficulty identifying ordinal positions through fifth,

then have five children line up and call out their positions in order.

Do you understand? *How do you describe the order of five things in a row?* [I start at the beginning of the row and use order words. I use the words *first, second, third, fourth,* and *fifth.*]

Reteaching Have children mime different instruments in a marching parade. Identify a position, first through fifth, and an action. For example, *Linda is first and plays the drums.* Children line up in order and march, miming their instruments.

Directions Have children color the third duck yellow, the fifth duck red, the first duck green, second duck orange, and the fourth duck blue.

Topic 2 • Lesson 8

ELL
STRATEGY
Visual
Learning

Visual Learning Animation

www.pearsonsuccessnet.com or CD

How many ladybugs do you see? [5] *What color is the fifth ladybug?* [Purple] *How can we say the order of the five ladybugs?* [First, second, third, fourth, fifth]

...ctions Have children: **2.** Circle the fourth butterfly. **3.** Circle the fifth hummingbird. **4.** Circle the third bee.

thirty-eight   38

Additional Activity

Simon Says

🕐 15 min 🏃

- Have 5 children line up and use ordinal numbers to call out their positions.
- Play Simon Says using ordinal numbers in your directions. For example: *Simon says the second person in line hops 2 times. Simon says the third person claps 3 times.*
- Repeat the game several times with different children.

---

3   Independent Practice

Children circle pictures in the fourth position, fifth position, and third position.

Close

Essential Understanding Numbers can be used to tell order (ordinal numbers). Positions/order in a row can be found by counting, and ordinal names, are similar to number names. *Remember that counting starts at the beginning of a row.*

ASSESSMENT

Exercise 1 is worth 1 point.
Use the rubric to score Exercise 2.

Exercise 2

Reason Abstractly Children should color the fourth tractor red and the fifth tractor blue.

ELL Use Repetition For children who need additional help, provide many opportunities to use ordinal position words.

Student Samples
3-point answer Children correctly identify the fourth and fifth tractors.

2-point answer Children incorrectly identify the ordinal position of one tractor.

1-point answer Children use incorrect colors to identify the ordinal position of two tractors.

Formative Assessment

Use the **Quick Check** to assess children's understanding.

Prescription for Differentiated Instruction
Use children's work on the **Quick Check** to prescribe differentiated instruction.

Points	Prescription
0–2	Intervention
3	On-Level
4	Advanced

Differentiated Instruction

Intervention

Musical Chairs

⏱ 10 min 👥

Materials 5 chairs numbered 1 to 5

- Have groups of 5 children play a game of "Musical Chairs" by walking around the chairs as music plays. When the music stops, ask children to sit in the closest chair.

- Have children take turns describing their positions with ordinals, starting with the child in the first chair. Repeat several times.

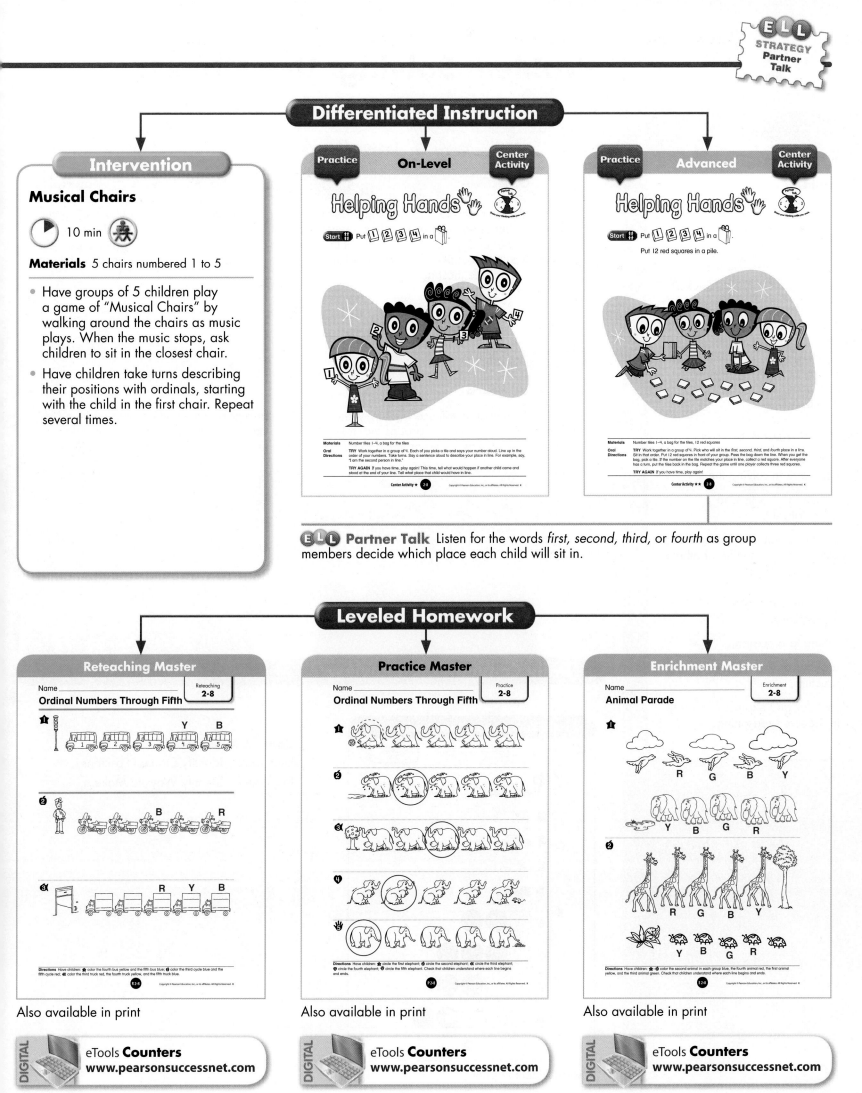

Practice — **On-Level** — **Center Activity**

Helping Hands ✋

Start Put ⟦1⟧⟦2⟧⟦3⟧⟦4⟧ in a 🎁

Materials Number tiles 1–4, a bag for the tiles

Oral Directions **TRY** Work together in a group of 4. Each of you picks a tile and says your number aloud. Line up in the order of your numbers. Take turns. Say a sentence aloud to describe your place in line. For example, say, "I am the second person in line."

TRY AGAIN If you have time, play again! This time, tell what would happen if another child came and stood at the end of your line. Tell what place that child would have in line.

Center Activity ★ 2-8

Practice — **Advanced** — **Center Activity**

Helping Hands ✋

Start Put ⟦1⟧⟦2⟧⟦3⟧⟦4⟧ in a 🎁
Put 12 red squares in a pile.

Materials Number tiles 1–4, a bag for the tiles, 12 red squares

Oral Directions **TRY** Work together in a group of 4. Pick who will sit in the first, second, third, and fourth place in a line. Sit in that order. Put 12 red squares in front of your group. Pass the bag down the line. When you get the bag, pick a tile. If the number on the tile matches your place in line, collect a red square. After everyone has a turn, put the tiles back in the bag. Repeat the game until one player collects three red squares.

TRY AGAIN If you have time, play again!

Center Activity ★★ 2-8

ELL Partner Talk Listen for the words *first, second, third,* or *fourth* as group members decide which place each child will sit in.

Leveled Homework

Reteaching Master

Name _____
Ordinal Numbers Through Fifth

Reteaching 2-8

Directions Have children: ★ color the fourth bus yellow and the fifth bus blue; ✦ color the third cycle blue and the fifth cycle red; ✤ color the third truck red, the fourth truck yellow, and the fifth truck blue.

R 2-8

Practice Master

Name _____
Ordinal Numbers Through Fifth

Practice 2-8

Directions Have children: ★ circle the first elephant; ✦ circle the second elephant; ✤ circle the third elephant; ✜ circle the fourth elephant; ✧ circle the fifth elephant. Check that children understand where each line begins and ends.

P 2-8

Enrichment Master

Name _____
Animal Parade

Enrichment 2-8

Directions Have children: ★–✦ color the second animal in each group blue, the fourth animal red, the first animal yellow, and the third animal green. Check that children understand where each line begins and ends.

E 2-8

Also available in print

Also available in print

Also available in print

eTools **Counters**
www.pearsonsuccessnet.com

eTools **Counters**
www.pearsonsuccessnet.com

eTools **Counters**
www.pearsonsuccessnet.com

Problem Solving: Use Objects

 **Lesson Overview**

Common Core

Domain
Counting and Cardinality

Cluster
Comparing numbers

Standards
K.CC.6 Identify whether the number of objects in one group is greater than, less than, or equal to the number of objects in another group, e.g., by using matching and counting strategies. Also **K.CC.4.b, K.CC.4.c**

Mathematical Practices

☑ Make sense of problems and persevere in solving them.

☑ Reason abstractly and quantitatively.

○ Construct viable arguments and critique the reasoning of others.

○ Model with mathematics.

☑ Use appropriate tools strategically.

○ Attend to precision.

○ Look for and make use of structure.

☑ Look for and express regularity in repeated reasoning.

Objective	Essential Understanding	Vocabulary	Materials
Children will use objects to show the number in each group, order the number of objects in each group, and identify the group that has the most or fewest number of objects.	Some problems can be solved by using objects to act out the actions in the problem.	**fewest** **most**	Connecting cubes (red, green, blue, yellow, purple, orange), crayons

PROFESSIONAL DEVELOPMENT

Math Background

In this lesson, children will use what they know about equal groups to order groups that have more or fewer objects. Children need to utilize the concept of one-to-one correspondence to determine which group has the most number of objects or the fewest number of objects.

1 Daily Common Core Review

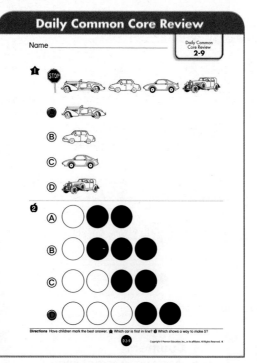

Content Reviewed

Exercise 1   Identify Ordinal Positions
Exercise 2   Identify Ways to Make 5

Also available in print

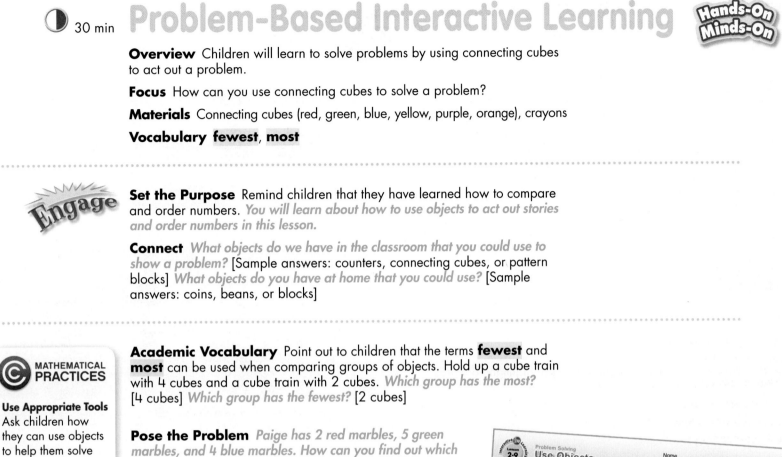

◑ 30 min **Problem-Based Interactive Learning**

Hands-On
Minds-On

Overview Children will learn to solve problems by using connecting cubes to act out a problem.

Focus How can you use connecting cubes to solve a problem?

Materials Connecting cubes (red, green, blue, yellow, purple, orange), crayons

Vocabulary fewest, most

Engage

Set the Purpose Remind children that they have learned how to compare and order numbers. *You will learn about how to use objects to act out stories and order numbers in this lesson.*

Connect *What objects do we have in the classroom that you could use to show a problem?* [Sample answers: counters, connecting cubes, or pattern blocks] *What objects do you have at home that you could use?* [Sample answers: coins, beans, or blocks]

MATHEMATICAL
PRACTICES

Use Appropriate Tools
Ask children how they can use objects to help them solve problems.

Academic Vocabulary Point out to children that the terms **fewest** and **most** can be used when comparing groups of objects. Hold up a cube train with 4 cubes and a cube train with 2 cubes. *Which group has the most?* [4 cubes] *Which group has the fewest?* [2 cubes]

Pose the Problem *Paige has 2 red marbles, 5 green marbles, and 4 blue marbles. How can you find out which group has the most?* Have children share their ideas.

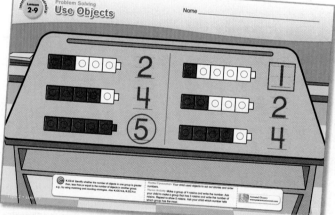

Model *We can use connecting cubes to find out which group of marbles has the most. How many red marbles does Paige have?* [2] Tell children to make a cube train with 2 red connecting cubes. *Paige has 5 green marbles. How many connecting cubes do we need to show the group of green marbles?* [5] Have children make a cube train with 5 green connecting cubes. *How many blue marbles does Paige have?* [4] Have children make a cube train with 4 blue connecting cubes. Count the cubes together. *How can we find out which group has the fewest marbles?* [Order the cube trains] Have children order the cube trains on the page from least to greatest. Then have them color the cubes in each row to match the cube trains and write the numbers that tell how many are in each group. *Which group has the fewest number of marbles?* [Red marbles] *Which group of marbles has the most?* [Green marbles] *Circle the number that tells which group has the most. What number did you circle?* [5]

Small Group Interaction Have partners work together to complete the student page as they listen to another story about Paige. *Paige has 1 yellow ball, 4 purple balls, and 2 orange balls. Which group of balls has the fewest?* [Yellow]

Extend

How many more green marbles than blue marbles does Paige have? [1 more] *How many fewer orange balls than purple balls does Paige have?* [2 fewer]

DIGITAL   eTools **Counters**
www.pearsonsuccessnet.com

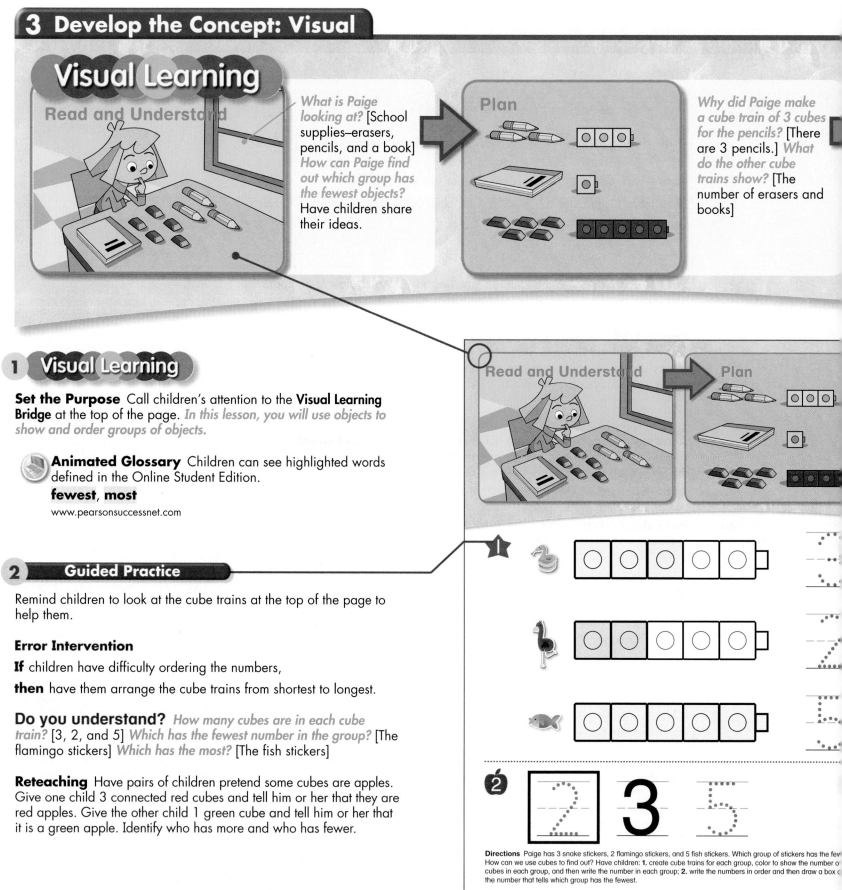

Visual Learning

Read and Understand

What is Paige looking at? [School supplies–erasers, pencils, and a book] *How can Paige find out which group has the fewest objects?* Have children share their ideas.

Plan

Why did Paige make a cube train of 3 cubes for the pencils? [There are 3 pencils.] *What do the other cube trains show?* [The number of erasers and books]

1 Visual Learning

Set the Purpose Call children's attention to the **Visual Learning Bridge** at the top of the page. *In this lesson, you will use objects to show and order groups of objects.*

Animated Glossary Children can see highlighted words defined in the Online Student Edition.

fewest, most

www.pearsonsuccessnet.com

2 Guided Practice

Remind children to look at the cube trains at the top of the page to help them.

Error Intervention

If children have difficulty ordering the numbers,

then have them arrange the cube trains from shortest to longest.

Do you understand? *How many cubes are in each cube train?* [3, 2, and 5] *Which has the fewest number in the group?* [The flamingo stickers] *Which has the most?* [The fish stickers]

Reteaching Have pairs of children pretend some cubes are apples. Give one child 3 connected red cubes and tell him or her that they are red apples. Give the other child 1 green cube and tell him or her that it is a green apple. Identify who has more and who has fewer.

Directions Paige has 3 snake stickers, 2 flamingo stickers, and 5 fish stickers. Which group of stickers has the few[est]? How can we use cubes to find out? Have children: **1.** create cube trains for each group, color to show the number o[f] cubes in each group, and then write the number in each group; **2.** write the numbers in order and then draw a box [around] the number that tells which group has the fewest.

Topic 2 • Lesson 9

Solve

☐ I

○○○ 3

○○○○○ 5

What did Paige do next? [She put the cube trains in order from fewest to most.] *Which group has the fewest objects?* [The group of books]

Look Back and Check

I

3

5

How does Paige look back and check? [She thinks about the number of each object in order from fewest to most.]

olve

I

○○ 3

○○○○ 5

Look Back and Check

I

3

5

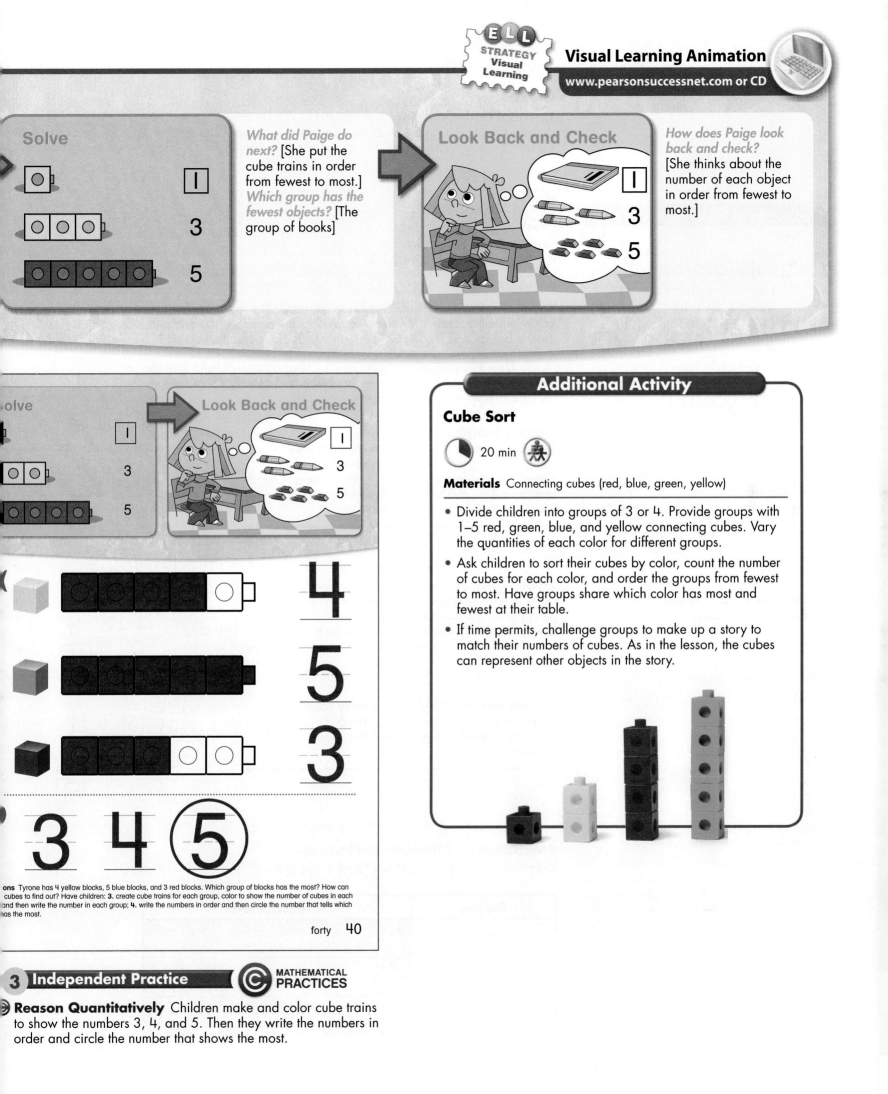

4

5

3

3   4   ⑤

ons Tyrone has 4 yellow blocks, 5 blue blocks, and 3 red blocks. Which group of blocks has the most? How can
cubes to find out? Have children: **3.** create cube trains for each group, color to show the number of cubes in each
and then write the number in each group; **4.** write the numbers in order and then circle the number that tells which
has the most.

forty **40**

3 Independent Practice   ⒸMATHEMATICAL PRACTICES

Reason Quantitatively Children make and color cube trains to show the numbers 3, 4, and 5. Then they write the numbers in order and circle the number that shows the most.

Additional Activity

Cube Sort

🕐 20 min 👥

Materials Connecting cubes (red, blue, green, yellow)

• Divide children into groups of 3 or 4. Provide groups with 1–5 red, green, blue, and yellow connecting cubes. Vary the quantities of each color for different groups.

• Ask children to sort their cubes by color, count the number of cubes for each color, and order the groups from fewest to most. Have groups share which color has most and fewest at their table.

• If time permits, challenge groups to make up a story to match their numbers of cubes. As in the lesson, the cubes can represent other objects in the story.

40A

Close

Essential Understanding Some problems can be solved by using objects to act out the actions in the problem. *Remember, you can use objects to identify the group with the most or fewest number of objects.*

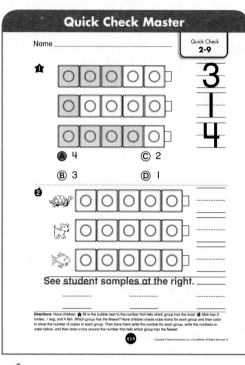

Formative Assessment

Use the **Quick Check** to assess children's understanding.

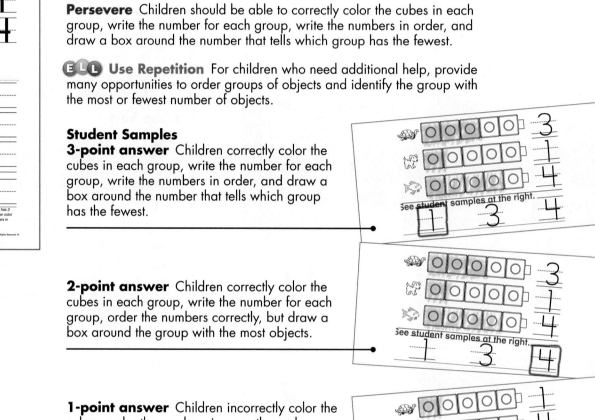

ASSESSMENT

Exercise 1 is worth 1 point.
Use the rubric to score Exercise 2.

Exercise 2

Persevere Children should be able to correctly color the cubes in each group, write the number for each group, write the numbers in order, and draw a box around the number that tells which group has the fewest.

ELL Use Repetition For children who need additional help, provide many opportunities to order groups of objects and identify the group with the most or fewest number of objects.

Student Samples
3-point answer Children correctly color the cubes in each group, write the number for each group, write the numbers in order, and draw a box around the number that tells which group has the fewest.

2-point answer Children correctly color the cubes in each group, write the number for each group, order the numbers correctly, but draw a box around the group with the most objects.

1-point answer Children incorrectly color the cubes, order the numbers incorrectly, and incorrectly identify the group with the fewest number of objects.

Prescription for Differentiated Instruction

Use children's work on the **Quick Check** to prescribe differentiated instruction.

Points	Prescription
0–2	Intervention
3	On-Level
4	Advanced

Differentiated Instruction

Intervention

Classmate Comparisons

⏱ 10 min 🧍

- Have between 0 to 5 boys come to the front of the room. Count how many. Write the number on the board next to the word *boys*.
- Have between 0 to 5 girls come to the front of the room. Count how many. Write the number on the board next to the word *girls*.
- Have children identify the group with the most children.

Practice | **On-Level** | **Center Activity**

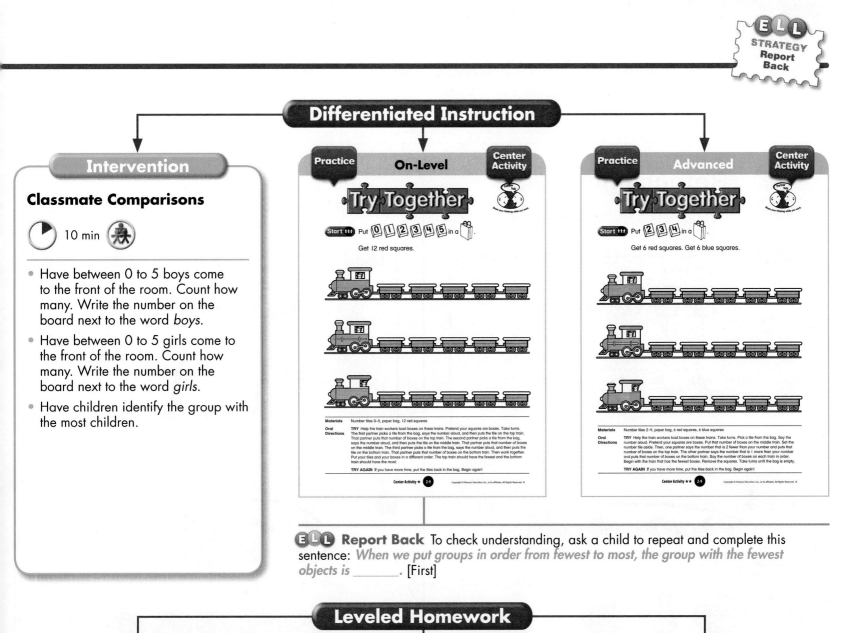

Start ↑↑↑ Put [0][1][2][3][4][5] in a 🛍.

Get 12 red squares.

Materials Number tiles 0–5, paper bag, 12 red squares

Oral Directions **TRY** Help the train workers load boxes on these trains. Pretend your squares are boxes. Take turns. The first partner picks a tile from the bag, says the number aloud, and then puts the tile on the top train. That partner puts that number of boxes on the top train. The second partner picks a tile from the bag, says the number aloud, and then puts the tile on the middle train. That partner puts that number of boxes on the middle train. The third partner picks a tile from the bag, says the number aloud, and puts the tile on the bottom train. That partner puts that number of boxes on the bottom train. Then work together. Put your tiles and your boxes in a different order. The top train should have the fewest and the bottom train should have the most.

TRY AGAIN If you have more time, put the tiles back in the bag. Begin again!

Center Activity ★ 2-9   Copyright © Pearson Education, Inc., or its affiliates. All Rights Reserved. K

Practice | **Advanced** | **Center Activity**

Start ↑↑↑ Put [2][3][4] in a 🛍.

Get 6 red squares. Get 6 blue squares.

Materials Number tiles 2–4, paper bag, 6 red squares, 6 blue squares

Oral Directions **TRY** Help the train workers load boxes on these trains. Take turns. Pick a tile from the bag. Say the number aloud. Pretend your squares are boxes. Put that number on the middle train. Set the number tile aside. Then, one partner says the number that is 2 fewer than your number and puts that number of boxes on the top train. The other partner says the number that is 1 more than your number and puts that number of boxes on the bottom train. Say the number as each train in order. Begin with the train that has the fewest boxes. Remove the squares. Take turns until the bag is empty.

TRY AGAIN If you have more time, put the tiles back in the bag. Begin again!

Center Activity ★★ 2-9   Copyright © Pearson Education, Inc., or its affiliates. All Rights Reserved. K

ELL Report Back To check understanding, ask a child to repeat and complete this sentence: *When we put groups in order from fewest to most, the group with the fewest objects is _____.* [First]

Leveled Homework

Reteaching Master

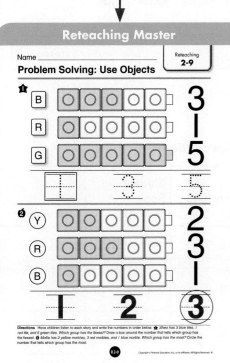

Name _____ Reteaching 2-9

Problem Solving: Use Objects

Directions Have children listen to each story and write the numbers in order below. ★ Shea has 3 blue tiles, 1 red tile, and 5 green tiles. Which group has the fewest? Draw a box around the number that tells which group has the fewest. ② Mollie has 2 yellow marbles, 3 red marbles, and 1 blue marble. Which group has the most? Circle the number that tells which group has the most.

R 2-9   Copyright © Pearson Education, Inc., or its affiliates. All Rights Reserved. K

Also available in print

DIGITAL
MindPoint Quiz Show
Comparing and Ordering 0 to 5
www.pearsonsuccessnet.com

Practice Master

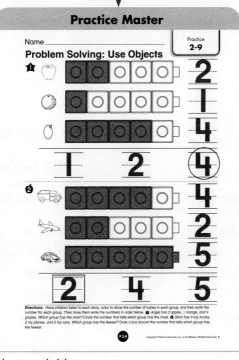

Name _____ Practice 2-9

Problem Solving: Use Objects

Directions Have children listen to each story, color to show the number of cubes in each group, and then write the number for each group. Then have them write the numbers in order below. ★ Angel has 2 apples, 1 orange, and 4 grapes. Which group has the most? Circle the number that tells which group has the most. ② Shon has 4 toy trucks, 2 toy planes, and 5 toy cars. Which group has the fewest? Draw a box around the number that tells which group has the fewest.

P 2-9   Copyright © Pearson Education, Inc., or its affiliates. All Rights Reserved. K

Also available in print

DIGITAL
eTools Counters
www.pearsonsuccessnet.com

Enrichment Master

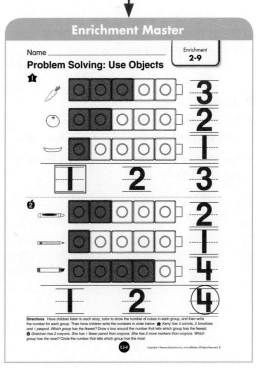

Name _____ Enrichment 2-9

Problem Solving: Use Objects

Directions Have children listen to each story, color to show the number of cubes in each group, and then write the number for each group. Then have children write the numbers in order below. ★ Kerry has 3 carrots, 2 tomatoes, and 1 peapod. Which group has the fewest? Draw a box around the number that tells which group has the fewest. ② Gretchen has 2 crayons. She has 1 fewer pencil than crayons. She has 2 more markers than crayons. Which group has the most? Circle the number that tells which group has the most.

E 2-9   Copyright © Pearson Education, Inc., or its affiliates. All Rights Reserved. K

Also available in print

DIGITAL
eTools Counters
www.pearsonsuccessnet.com

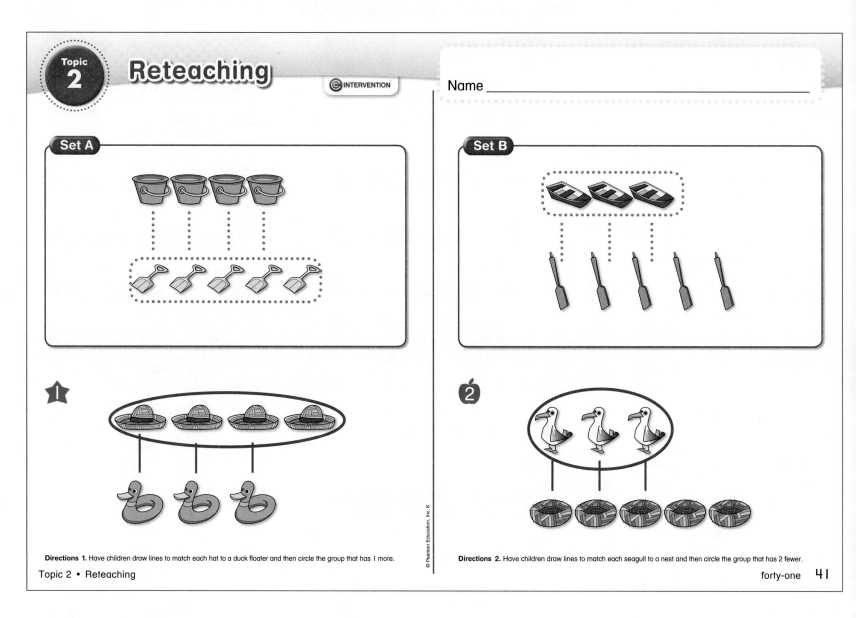

Purpose

- Provide children with more examples and practice for each lesson in the topic.
- For intervention, use the resources listed in the chart to the right.

Item Analysis for Diagnosis and Intervention

Objective	© Common Core Standards	Reteaching Sets	Student Book Lessons	Intervention
Identify 1 or 2 more.	**K.CC.6**	Set A	2-2	A-2
Identify 1 or 2 fewer.	**K.CC.6**	Set B	2-3	A-2
Write numerals in order.	**K.CC.4.c**	Set C	2-7	A-11
Identify ordinal positions.	**K.CC.2**	Set D	2-8	A-22

Topic 2 — Reteaching

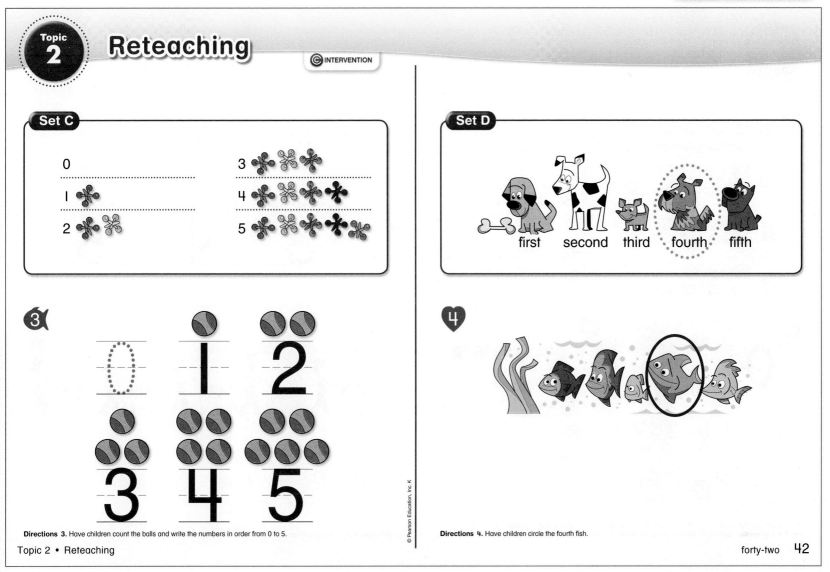

Set C

0		3
1		4
2		5

Set D

first   second   third   fourth   fifth

0   1   2

3   4   5

Directions 3. Have children count the balls and write the numbers in order from 0 to 5.

Directions 4. Have children circle the fourth fish.

Topic 2 • Reteaching

Response to Intervention

RTI
TIER **1** ONGOING

Ongoing Intervention
- Lessons with guiding questions to assess understanding
- Support to prevent misconceptions and to reteach

RTI
TIER **2** STRATEGIC

Strategic Intervention
- Targeted to small groups who need more support
- Easy to implement

RTI
TIER **3** INTENSIVE

Intensive Intervention
- Instruction to accelerate progress
- Instruction focused on foundational skills

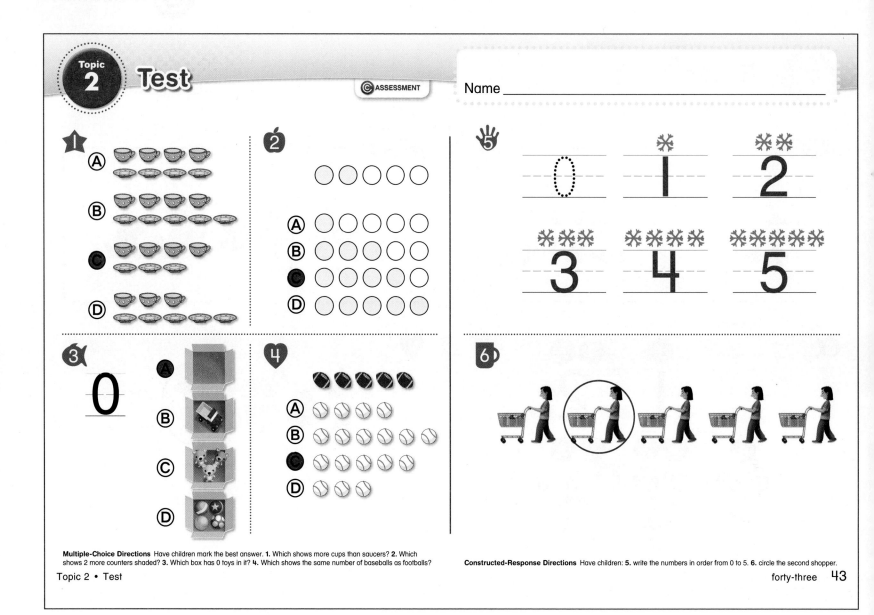

Name _____

Multiple-Choice Directions Have children mark the best answer. **1.** Which shows more cups than saucers? **2.** Which shows 2 more counters shaded? **3.** Which box has 0 toys in it? **4.** Which shows the same number of baseballs as footballs?

Constructed-Response Directions Have children: **5.** write the numbers in order from 0 to 5. **6.** circle the second shopper.

Topic 2 • Test

forty-three 43

Purpose

- Assess children's understanding of the concepts and skills in Topic 2 using multiple-choice and constructed-response formats.

- Additional assessment options can be found in the Teacher Resource Masters.

- For intervention materials that correspond to all tests, use the resources listed in the chart to the right.

Test-Taking Tips

Discuss with children the following tips for test success.

Understand the Question
- Look for important words.
- Turn the question into a statement: "I need to find out..."

Gather Information
- Get information from text.
- Get information from pictures, maps, diagrams, tables, and graphs.

Make a Plan
- Think about problem-solving skills and strategies.
- Choose computation methods.

Make Smart Choices
- Eliminate wrong answers.
- Try working backward from an answer.
- Check answers for reasonableness; estimate.

Item Analysis for Diagnosis and Intervention

Objective	Common Core Standards	Test Items	Student Book Lessons	Intervention System
Compare groups of objects and identify which group has *more*, *fewer*, or the *same* number as the other group.	K.CC.6	1,2,4	2-1, 2-2, 2-3, 2-6, 2-9	A-2
Understand that *zero* means *none*.	K.CC.3	3	2-4, 2-5	A-1
Write numerals in order.	K.CC.4.c	5	2-7	A-11
Identify ordinal positions.	K.CC.4	6	2-8	A-22

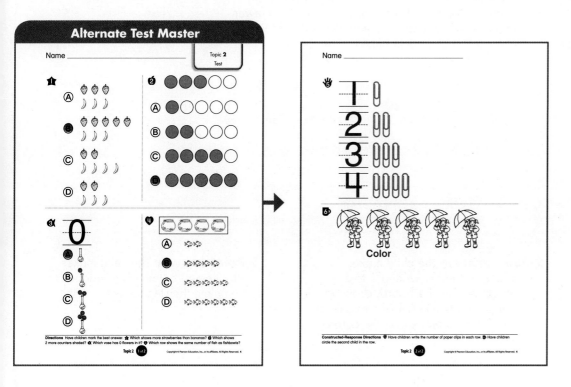

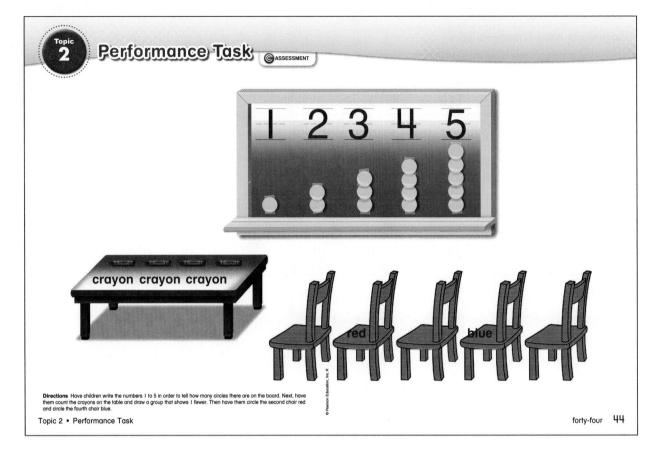

1 2 3 4 5

crayon crayon crayon

red   blue

Directions Have children write the numbers 1 to 5 in order to tell how many circles there are on the board. Next, have them count the crayons on the table and draw a group that shows 1 fewer. Then have them circle the second chair red and circle the fourth chair blue.

© Pearson Education, Inc. K

Topic 2 • Performance Task   forty-four **44**

Purpose Assess children's understanding of the concepts and skills in Topic 2 through a performance-based task.

Task For this assessment, children write numbers in order, draw a group with 1 fewer, and identify ordinal positions.

Get Ready Review with children that they have learned how to write numbers and compare groups of objects to tell which has more or fewer. Review and count ordinal numbers.

Guiding the Activity Make sure children write the numbers 1 to 5, draw a group of crayons, and circle the chairs according to ordinal position.

Questioning Strategies How many circles are there in each stack? How many crayons did you draw on the table? Which group shows fewer objects? Which chair will you circle in red? Which chair will you circle in blue?

Scoring Rubric

3-Point answer The child writes 1 to 5 consecutively on the board, draws the appropriate number of crayons, and colors the second chair red and the fourth chair blue.

2-Point answer The child makes a mistake on either writing 1 to 5 consecutively on the board, drawing the appropriate number of crayons, or coloring the correct chairs the correct color.

1-Point answer The child makes an attempt, but needs assistance to complete the steps of the activity.